# Transactions
## of the
## Royal
## Historical
## Society

SIXTH SERIES

# XXXI

CAMBRIDGE
UNIVERSITY PRESS

Published by the Press Syndicate of the University of Cambridge
University Printing House, Shaftesbury Road, Cambridge CB2 8BS,
United Kingdom
One Liberty Plaza, Floor 20, New York, NY 10006, USA
477 Williamstown Road, Port Melbourne, VIC 3207, Australia
C/Orense, 4, Planta 13, 28020 Madrid, Spain
Lower Ground Floor, Nautica Building, The Water Club,
Beach Road, Granger Bay, 8005 Cape Town, South Africa

First published 2021

*A catalogue record for this book is available from the British Library*

ISBN 9781009177344 hardback

SUBSCRIPTIONS. The serial publications of the Royal Historical Society, *Royal Historical Society Transactions* (ISSN 0080-4401) and Camden Fifth Series (ISSN 0960-1163) volumes, may be purchased together on annual subscription. The 2021 subscription price, which includes print and electronic access (but not VAT), is £222 (US $371 in the USA, Canada, and Mexico) and includes Camden Fifth Series, volumes 61, 62 and Transactions Sixth Series, volume 31 (published in December). The electronic-only price available to institutional subscribers is £186 (US $310 in the USA, Canada, and Mexico). Japanese prices are available from Kinokuniya Company Ltd, PO Box 55, Chitose, Tokyo 156, Japan. EU subscribers may be required to pay import VAT at their country's rate on receipt of physical deliveries. EU subscribers for electronic deliveries who are not VAT registered should add VAT at their country's rate. VAT registered subscribers should provide their VAT number. Prices include delivery by air.

Subscription orders, which must be accompanied by payment, may be sent to a bookseller, subscription agent, or direct to the publisher: Cambridge University Press, University Printing House, Shaftesbury Road, Cambridge CB2 8BS, UK; or in the USA, Canada, and Mexico: Cambridge University Press, Journals Fulfillment Department, One Liberty Plaza, Floor 20, New York, NY 10006, USA.

SINGLE VOLUMES AND BACK VOLUMES. A list of Royal Historical Society volumes available from Cambridge University Press may be obtained from the Humanities Marketing Department at the address above.

*Printed in the UK by Bell & Bain Ltd, Glasgow*

# CONTENTS

PAGE

Presidential Address: Material Turns in British History: IV.
    Empire in India, Cancel Cultures and the Country House    1
    Margot C. Finn

Responding to Violence: Liturgy, Authority and Sacred
    Places, c. 900–c. 1150    23
    Sarah Hamilton

Baroque around the Clock: Daniello Bartoli SJ (1608–1685)
    and the Uses of Global History    49
    Simon Ditchfield

What Happens when a Written Constitution is Printed?
    A History across Boundaries    75
    Linda Colley

An Ottoman Arab Man of Letters and the Meanings of
    Empire, c. 1860    89
    Andrew Arsan

Revisiting RHS's 'Race, Ethnicity & Equality in UK
    History: A Report and Resource for Change'    115
    Shahmima Akhtar

*Transactions of the RHS* 31 (2021), pp. 1–21 © The Author(s), 2021. Published by Cambridge University Press on behalf of the Royal Historical Society
doi:10.1017/S0080440121000013

TRANSACTIONS OF THE

# ROYAL HISTORICAL SOCIETY

PRESIDENTIAL ADDRESS

## By Margot C. Finn

## MATERIAL TURNS IN BRITISH HISTORY: IV. EMPIRE IN INDIA, CANCEL CULTURES AND THE COUNTRY HOUSE

READ 27 NOVEMBER 2020

ABSTRACT. This lecture seeks to historicise the so-called cancel culture associated with the 'culture wars' waged in Britain in *c.* 2020. Focusing on empire and on the domestic, British impacts of Georgian-era imperial material cultures, it argues that dominant proponents of these 'culture wars' in the public sphere fundamentally distort the British pasts they vociferously claim to preserve and defend. By failing to acknowledge the extent to which eighteenth- and nineteenth-century British men and women themselves contested imperial expansion under the aegis of the East India Company – and decried its impact on British material culture, including iconic stately homes – twenty-first-century exponents of culture wars who rail against the present-day rise of histories of race and empire in the heritage sector themselves erase key layers of British experience. In so doing, they impoverish public understanding of the past.

This is my fourth lecture for the Royal Historical Society on 'Material Turns in British History', exploring how attention to colonial and material cultures can enhance our understanding of the British past. It has been composed in what can only be described as historic times. Against a backdrop of environmental calamity and amidst a global epidemiological crisis, historians labour today in the throes of a so-called culture war, in which empire and colonialism are key protagonists. 'Cancel cultures' are conspicuous in the armoury of this cultural conflict. '*Cancel culture* refers to the popular practice of withdrawing support for (cancelling) public figures and companies after they have done or said something considered objectionable or offensive,' the *Pop Culture Dictionary* explains. '*Cancel culture* is generally discussed as being performed on social media in the form of group shaming.'[1] History

---

[1] *Pop Culture Dictionary*, www.dictionary.com/e/pop-culture/cancel-culture. Similarly, the online Cambridge dictionary defines cancel culture as 'a way of behaving in a society or group, especially on social media, in which it is common to completely reject and stop

has come under repeated fire from all political sides and generational cohorts in this heady atmosphere. In this lecture, I trace a few highly visible threads among the rich tapestry of this contemporary conflict and seek, by locating the British country house within histories of imperialism, to situate today's 'culture wars' in both a broader and a longer historical context.

My lecture is in three main parts. I begin with a sweeping, and necessarily schematic, survey of today's *soi-disant* culture war in Britain, focusing on its dominant timelines and cast of characters and noting the peculiar erasure of the East India Company (EIC) that characterises social-media enabled debates about British imperialism. I turn in the next two sections to the closely entwined histories of the East India Company and the British country house, suggesting that erasure and selective historical amnesia – cancelling, if you will – were woven into the history of the stately home in the Georgian and early Victorian years in ways that prefigure twentieth- and twenty-first-century repressions and reimaginings of empire in the public and the scholarly imaginations. In my conclusion, I return to our contemporary culture war, underlining the need to push beyond facile conceptions of the past that 'cancel' or deny earlier generations' participation in robust, contentious debates about the domestic impact of Britain's empire. Not only school and university curriculums, museums, and cultural organisations such as the National Trust, but also commercial venues, the Church of England, the military and representatives of the monarchy are now caught up in the legacies of this contested heritage.[2] If we are to engage intelligently with these debates, I suggest, it behoves us to acknowledge and understand their extended, conflicted genealogy.

## I Culture war(s)?

Do we live in times riven by one or more 'culture wars'? The popular press, some politicians and many Twitter users are convinced that we do. Their conviction resounds from the pages of the *Daily Mail*, which locates the key battlefields of the culture war in identity politics – most notably in claims for racial equality that have been brought to the forefront of public consciousness by Black Lives Matter. Reporting in June

supporting someone because they have said or done something that offends you': https://dictionary.cambridge.org/dictionary/english/cancel-culture. Both sources accessed 9 July 2021.

[2] Abundant evidence of the diverse stakeholders caught up in the 'culture wars' can be found in the webpages of Policy Exchange's 'History Matters' project, discussed below. At the time of this lecture's delivery, Policy Exchange had published four 'editions' of material for this project. At the time of finalising this text, nine editions had been published: https://policyexchange.org.uk/history-matters-project, accessed 9 July 2021.

2020 that the prime minister had selected Munira Mirza to set up his new race commission, the *Mail* proclaimed 'No10 "declares war on woke": Boris Johnson "is taking on cultural battles over statues to shore up Tory base"'.[3] As monuments to local worthies and national icons have toppled from (or trembled on) their pedestals, History and History's alleged cancellation have loomed increasingly large in this narrative of cultural Armageddon. September 2020 saw the actor Laurence Fox announce his determination to launch a new political party, in the aftermath of his assertion that pervasive discussions of racism in the media were 'boring'. The *Daily Mail*'s report of Fox's initiative quoted his claim that 'The people of the United Kingdom are tired of being told that we represent the very thing we have, in history, stood together against,' noting his objective of 'celebrating Britain's cultural history' in the face of such critiques.[4]

In newspapers, on Twitter, and within both houses of Parliament, 'culture war' and 'cancel culture' are now bandied about by Conservative commentators as signifiers of all that is wrong with a section of the public they identify as a cacophonous minority opposed to the 'common sense' traditionalism of a silent majority. The revival of large-scale anti-racism protest in Britain in the aftermath of the killing of George Floyd on 25 May 2020 has both accelerated this conflict and focused it increasingly on histories of empire, race and nation. In July 2020, Conservative MP Sir John Hayes launched the 'Common Sense' group of MPs and peers to 'deliver on the Conservative pledge to control immigration and so keep faith with blue collar Tory voters'.[5] By September, *The Times* was reporting that members of this new assemblage had joined forces with the European Research Group to refuse 'unconscious bias training intended to tackle racism in the Commons, accusing parliamentary authorities of "pandering to the woke agenda" … "I would rather gouge my eyes out with a blunt stick than sit through that Marxist, snake oil crap," said one.'[6] As Ben Bradley – newly elected Conservative MP for Mansfield, self-professed 'first blue brick in the red wall' and unconscious-bias-training refusenik – tweeted in October,

---

[3] *Daily Mail*, 16 June 2020.

[4] 'Some REAL opposition? Laurence Fox to launch new political party to fight "culture wars" with £5million from former Tory donors – as Nigel Farage threatens to launch his own anti-lockdown party' (*Daily Mail*, 27 September 2020). See similarly 'Megxit? It's Brexit all over again! Just when we thought Britain was healing, a new cultural war is raging – but despite hysterical claims, it's NOT to do with racism, insists former equalities minister TREVOR PHILLIPS', *Daily Mail*, 17 January 2020.

[5] Sir John Hayes, MP, 'We need to stop misplacing common sense on immigration for bigotry, blasts Sir John Hayes', *The Express*, 5 July 2020.

[6] Esther Webber and Eleni Courea, 'Dozens of Tory MPs Set to Refuse Unconscious Bias Training', *The Times*, 21 September 2020.

'#CriticalRaceTheory and the #BLM organisation … are not an innocent anti racism campaign, it's political ideology and should be treated
as such!'[7]

More sober and sustained is the 'History Matters' campaign launched
by the centre-right think tank Policy Exchange in June 2020. Led by the
former chair of the Equality and Human Rights Commission, Trevor
Phillips, this project is guided by a panel of eleven 'historians, public
figures and people interested in history'. 'We all want to find ways to
improve the life opportunities and outcomes for people from BAME
backgrounds,' Phillips wrote in explaining the group's rationale. 'But
what concerns me about the current moment is the rapid and unthinking
way in which large swathes of our public heritage is [sic] being effectively
re-written, or erased entirely – much of it seemingly without much
proper debate or forethought.'[8] In both its visual iconography and its
straplines, 'History Matters' reflects wider claims that historians – like
turkeys voting for Christmas – are intent on cancelling History. Led
emblematically by Richard Lionheart, its advocates underline 'public
concern for the rewriting of history', assert that 'Two thirds of people
say judging our past with today's values is mistaken,' allege 'Rock
bottom support for removing historical statues, including Churchill'
and have issued a 'call for evidence as history becomes focus of culture
war'.[9]

These sentiments have travelled rapidly along the corridors of power,
with important ramifications for History in schools, universities and cultural organisations. In September, Oliver Dowden, the secretary of state
for digital, culture, media and sport, sent twenty-six cultural organisations in England a letter warning them against removing statues, or
other objects of contested cultural heritage, from public display at the
risk of losing their public funding.[10] In October, in a speech delivered
at the end of Black History Month, Kemi Badenoch, minister for equalities, asserted firmly that, in schools and universities, 'our curriculum
does not need decolonising' and warned that any school uncritically

[7] @BBradley_Mans (21 October 2020).
[8] https://policyexchange.org.uk/press-release/policy-exchange-launches-new-history-
project, accessed 12 November 2020. The choice of 'History Matters' as the rubric for this initiative may strike historians with a longer-term engagement with Black history as ironic: Professor
Hakim Adi of the University of Chichester established a 'History Matters' coalition in 2014 with
quite different assumptions and goals: www.younghistoriansproject.org/single-post/2019/03/
15/Life-and-times-of-Britains-first-black-History-professor-Hakim-Adi-Part-II.
[9] https://policyexchange.org.uk/press-release/policy-exchange-launches-new-history-project.
Policy Exchange features an image of the Grade II listed equestrian statue of Richard Lionheart
outside the Palace of Westminster with this text.
[10] 'Letter from Culture Secretary on HM Government position on contested heritage', 22
September 2020, www.gov.uk/government/publications/letter-from-culture-secretary-on-
hm-government-position-on-contested-heritage, accessed 9 July 2021.

teaching Critical Race Theory 'is breaking the law'.[11] In November, Conservative life peer Baroness Eaton intervened, 'To ask Her Majesty's Government what assessment they have made of steps taken by some universities to decolonise the history curriculum; and what plans they have to issue guidance to universities on making the history curriculum as previously taught available to students.'[12] That History not only matters but is also fundamentally *different* rings out from these debates. MPs and peers do not argue that the teaching of evolution in schools and universities must be balanced by creationist pedagogy, nor (thank goodness) do they suggest that compulsory relationship teaching on LGBT+ equality in primary schools must be matched by compulsory lessons on how to be homophobic. When it comes to History, however, science – in the sense of *Wissenschaft*, or the systematic pursuit of new knowledge – not only flies out the window, but is held up to ridicule and opprobrium. In the common parlance of our times, it is 'cancelled'.

What are the defining features of the History that proponents of this dominant paradigm of culture war propound? The Policy Exchange 'History Matters' project provides useful evidence for answering this question. In June 2020, the group established a webpage to register examples of Britain's 'culture war' under four main rubrics: Statue Removals, Name Changes, Apologies and 'Decolonising' the Curriculum. Three further 'editions' had augmented this rolling 'compendium' of evidence by 24 September 2020.[13] Adorned by images of government ministers, they add Art Symbols, Museums, Galleries and Institutions, Education, and Public Spaces to a roster that echoes lists of the war dead inscribed on memorial monuments.[14] The presentation of these data is unsystematic, and Policy Exchange offers no information on any selection criteria for inclusion or exclusion they have applied. Nonetheless, several salient features emerge from the ninety-nine entries. Material culture and the built environment feature prominently in 'History Matters'' understanding of History's pedagogic duty. In their first four editions, 24 per cent of their entries mention the renaming of

[11] Calvin Robinson, 'Kemi Badenoch is right to take on Critical Race Theory', *The Spectator*, 21 October 2020, www.spectator.co.uk/article/kemi-badenoch-is-right-to-take-on-critical-race-theory.

[12] 'Decolonising the History Curriculum', written question tabled 8 October 2020, House of Lords, [HL8921], https://lordsbusiness.parliament.uk/ItemOfBusiness?itemOfBusinessId=84702&sectionId=50&businessPaperDate=2020-10-09.

[13] The editions (3, 4 and 24 September 2020) are attributed to Alexander Gray, Research Fellow, Security and Extremism: https://policyexchange.org.uk/history-matters-project/page/4 and https://policyexchange.org.uk/history-matters-project/page/3, accessed 9 July 2021. The subsequent editions are dated 20 October 2020 to 9 April 2021.

[14] 'History Matters', first edition, 28 June 2020, https://policyexchange.org.uk/publication/history-matters-project, accessed 9 July 2021.

buildings, roads or schools, while 23 per cent mention public statues, busts or commemorative plaques. (In contrast, only 13 per cent reference the decolonisation of university curricula.)[15] The absence of women from this monumental vision of Britain's national history is a notable, but unremarked, characteristic of the 'History Matters' campaign: by default, the project's vision conceptualises history and heritage as inherently masculine domains.[16] Public monuments controlled by local councils dominated the first edition, but the project's fourth edition turned attention increasingly to cultural and educational organisations, renewing its 'call for evidence asking museum directors, curators, teachers and the wider public to share their experiences and concerns about the ways in which history is being politicised, and sometimes distorted'.[17]

The 'History Matters' group emphatically proclaims its own approach to the past to be free of politics. 'In cataloguing these examples, we do not offer any judgment on the actions of the individual or institution in question,' their website asserts. This claim sits uncomfortably with the group's conclusion, unchanged since it began to gather its evidence, that History today 'is the most active front in a new culture war, and that action is being taken widely and quickly in a way that does not reflect public opinion or growing concern over our treatment of the past'.[18] These conflicting statements rest uneasily on the compendium's evidence, much of which lacks the conventional referencing that would allow the reader to test its veracity.[19] Spot checks of the patchy references and cited texts do not always inspire confidence. Item 12 of the second edition, for example, is headed by the bold claim that 'More than 180 historians have called on the Home Office to remove the history element of the

---

[15] The unsystematic presentation of the Policy Exchange data renders precise analysis problematic.

[16] The hyper-masculine understanding of the past projected by 'History Matters' is reflected in the composition of its list of 'at risk' statues and busts. This includes Robert Baden-Powell, Lt Col. Benson, James Boulton, Sir John Cass, Joseph Chamberlain, Sir Robert Clive, Edward Colston, Viscount Combermere, Oliver Cromwell, Sir Robert Geffrye, Thomas Guy, Viscount Melville, Robert Milligan, Lord Nelson, Sir Robert Peel, Thomas Picton, General Sir Redvers Buller, Cecil Rhodes, Sir Hans Sloane and James Watt.

[17] https://policyexchange.org.uk/publication/history-matters-fourth-edition.

[18] Text cited from the introductory statements of the first and fourth editions, accessed 9 July 2021. Policy Exchange's approach to factual evidence has, more broadly, attracted critical comment. See for example responses to a 2019 Policy Exchange report on the 'crisis' of free speech at universities which wrongly claimed that Germaine Greer had been no-platformed at Cardiff University, a claim subsequently reported in the House of Commons: Anna Fazackerley, 'Gavin Williamson using "misleading" research to justify campus free-speech law', *The Guardian*, 27 February 2021.

[19] For example, citations to newspaper articles that lack dates (a problem exacerbated when the articles are located behind paywalls), the presence of broken hyperlinks and the absence of names of authors cited.

UK citizenship test.' Navigating beyond 'History Matters'' broken link to a mistitled '*History Journal*' that supposedly supports this claim, a persistent reader can view the offending letter in full via the *Guardian* website, as published in *History: The Official Journal of the Historical Association*. Here we learn that the 180 historians – of whom I am one – have not called for History to be removed from the Home Office test. Instead, they have requested that the factual errors with respect to the histories of slavery and empire (with which the current test is larded) be removed, rather than remaining compulsory learning for prospective UK citizens.[20]

Based on a tendentious evidence base, the 'History Matters' project is at least as illuminating for what it leaves out as for what it takes into its purview. The place of the East India Company in Britain's imperial pantheon is one of these many salient silences. Like the 50-ish per cent of the population that is female, over three centuries of British imperial expansion in South Asia are conspicuous for their absence from view.[21] A passing reference to Lord Adonis's desire to topple the statue of Robert Clive, and an (equally cursory) mention of a proposal by Ealing Council to rename Havelock Road as Guru Nanak Road appear to represent the full extent of India's place in the British empire, until the celebrated life of Winston Churchill heaves into view.[22]

Where EIC men do feature in the project's pantheon, their exploits in India are unacknowledged. Item 4 of the first edition of its compendium of evidence of a raging culture war fuelled by cancel culture, for example, instances Chester Council's discussion of whether to remove a large equestrian statue of Viscount Combermere from the city centre. 'Field Marshal Stapleton Cotton, 1st Viscount Combermere was a military leader, diplomat and politician and made a Field Marshal in 1855,' the website observes. 'He served under the Duke of Wellington in the Peninsular War.'[23] Absent from this analysis is the rationale for the debate on Combermere's statue: he served as governor of Barbados from 1817 to 1820 and was financially compensated for Parliament's emancipation of 420 enslaved persons on Nevis and St Kitts in 1834.[24]

---

[20] Item 12, second edition, https://policyexchange.org.uk/publication/history-matters-project-second-edition; the letter, posted on *History* 21 July 2020, can be accessed from: https://historyjournal.org.uk/2020/07/21/historians-call-for-a-review-of-home-office-citizenship-and-settlement-test.

[21] Queen Victoria and Elizabeth II are the only women (figured as statues/plaques rather than as persons) named in the ninety-nine entries. The ninety-nine entries mention far more than ninety-nine persons in total.

[22] Clive features in the first edition (item 9); Havelock in the second edition (item 2); Churchill (in the context both of the Bengal Famine of 1943 and of his opposition to Indian independence) in the second edition (item 26) and the fourth edition (item 13).

[23] First edition (item 4).

[24] 'Stapleton Cotton, 1st Viscount Combermere', in Legacies of British Slave-ownership database: www.ucl.ac.uk/lbs/person/view/25180, accessed 14 November 2020.

Also missing from this description of Combermere's valour is his career in India. A veteran of the Fourth Anglo-Mysore War, Combermere first met Wellington not in Europe but in the Madras Presidency, where both men established their military repute.[25] His full title reflects contemporary recognition of the central part that India played throughout his career. He was Viscount Combermere of Bhurtpore in the East Indies because, as commander-in-chief of India in the 1820s, he presided over the reduction of a Mahratta fort long held to be impregnable.[26] Selective amnesia regarding the East India Company's place in the wider fabric of the British empire is by no means peculiar to Policy Exchange's initiative.[27] Rather, it characterises wider public rememberings and forgettings of empire in India in our so-called culture war.

## II Empire men, the East India Company and the country house

Why does India in general and the East India Company in particular play such a limited role in present-day discussions of the British empire? Debates spurred by the Black Lives Matter movement unsurprisingly have focused attention on the slave systems of the Atlantic world, and the role played by slave-trading and slave-owning British men in upholding them. In turning attention to India, it is not my intention to efface those vitally important histories, but rather to locate them in a wider imperial system in which the Atlantic and Indian Ocean worlds were both entwined and mutually sustaining.[28] Combermere's biography, like his stately home in Cheshire, embodies this entanglement.

A Cistercian foundation established in the twelfth century, Combermere Abbey passed into the Cotton family with the dissolution of the monasteries. Newly knighted by Henry VIII, Sir George Cotton gained the abbey and its 22,000 acres in the 1540s, and promptly demolished its main buildings – a salutary reminder that processes of erasure have played an integral part in forging Britain's four nations for

[25] H. M. Chichester, revised by James Lunt, 'Cotton Stapleton, first Viscount Combermere (1773–1865)', *Oxford Dictionary of National Biography* (Oxford, 2004; 11 March 2021 edition).

[26] *Memoirs and Correspondence of Field Marshal Viscount Combermere, from His Family Papers*, ed. M. W. S. Cotton [Viscountess Combermere] and W. Knollys (2 vols., 1866), chs. 2–3.

[27] Subsequent to the delivery of this lecture, this point has been made especially forcibly by Sathnam Sanghera, *Empireland: How Imperialism Has Shaped Modern Britain* (2021), ch. 11, esp. 197.

[28] For the EIC's entanglement with Atlantic-world slavery, see Chris Jeppesen, 'East Meets West: Exploring the Connections between Britain, the Caribbean and the East India Company, c. 1757–1857', in *Britain's History and Memory of Transatlantic Slavery*, ed. Katie Donington, Ryan Hanley and Jessica Moody (Liverpool, 2016), 116–40.

centuries. The resulting Tudor manor house was remodelled by successive generations, obtaining its current, Gothic style at the behest of the
first viscount, in the aftermath of the Napoleonic wars.[29] Today the
abbey operates as a luxury wedding venue, 'Steeped in a thousand
years of English history'. What does it mean to be steeped in English
history? The 'History' tab of the Combermere Abbey website depicts
the English past as an insular national history, shorn as it is of references
to colonial wealth and imperial military exploits.[30] The high points of
that potted history offer a sharp contrast to the evidence presented to
the public by Combermere's family and friends in the Georgian and
Victorian eras. Here we find instead a man propelled into empire by
the profligate hospitality of his father, whose devotion to country pursuits
had forced the sale of family estates valued at £200,000 (or, over
£8 million in today's money).[31] Service as governor in Barbados (1817–20),
commander-in-chief of Ireland (1822–5) and commander-in-chief of
India (1825–30) clearly reflected Combermere's staunch conservative
values. 'Toryism has been for centuries an heirloom of the Cotton
family, and he cherished it with careful fidelity,' the Victorian biography
orchestrated by Combermere's family asserted. 'The British officer, he
thought, should be essentially conservative, as the guardian of established
rule and the enemy to changes which might implicate the chivalrous
loyalty to which he is sworn.'[32] But his imperial career was hardly an
innovation. His family's political and economic fortunes, including
their purchase of English landed estates, had, since the seventeenth
century, been predicated on ownership of sugar plantations and the
enslaved humans whose forced labour extracted profits from the four
Leeward Islands.[33]

While serving as governor of Barbados in the 1810s, Combermere
refashioned the abbey in Gothic style, installing a Wellington Wing to
commemorate the senior officer with whom he had served both at the
storming at Seringapatam in India in 1799 and later in the Peninsular
War. Inside the abbey, behind its new, mock-Gothic facade, the
impress of India is readily discerned in material culture acquired by

[29] Combermere Abbey Estate, https://combermereabbey.co.uk/history. See also www.
historichouses.org/houses/house-listing/combermere-abbey.html.

[30] https://combermereabbey.co.uk/history. High points include Henry VIII's dissolution
of the monasteries, 'extensive Gothic remodelling' from 1775 to 1820, the estate's purchase
by Sir Kenneth Crossley of Crossley Motors in 1919 and service as an evacuee girls' school
in World War II.

[31] www.ucl.ac.uk/lbs/person/view/25180.

[32] *Memoirs and Correspondence*, II, 376–7.

[33] This wealth, much augmented by intermarriage with women of the Caribbean planter
aristocracy, is delineated by J. R. V. Johnson, 'The Stapleton Sugar Plantations in the
Leeward Islands', *Bulletin of the John Rylands Library*, 48 (1965), 175–206.

the commonplace practices of empire in South Asia: conquest, gifting, loot and prize. Combermere was an adept practitioner of the acquisitive collecting practices associated with East India Company military campaigns.[34] Writing to the governor general, Lord Amherst, during the reduction of Bharatpur fort, he provided detailed military intelligence, interlaced with news of the items seized from the raja's palace that he was sending as gifts to Amherst, his wife and his daughter.[35] The treasure taken by his army was valued at £480,000 (in excess of £27 million today), of which £500 was expended to mount two brass field-pieces presented by the army to the commander-in-chief. '[T]hey now stand in a gallery [at Combermere Abbey] lined with armour and every description of weapon,' Mary, Viscountess Combermere and Captain Knollys reported in their *Memoirs and Correspondence* of Combermere in 1866.[36] Elevated to viscount for this victory, Combermere as commander-in-chief was entitled to one-eighth of the Bharatpur prize money, a hefty sum worth just under £3.5 million today.[37]

The months that followed this victory of 1826 saw Combermere travel throughout the Upper Provinces of Bengal, reviewing his troops, engaging in diplomacy with Indian princes and collecting artwork and armour for display at his English country house. Among the Indian princely states which the East India Company was, variously, using to shore up its power and seeking to supplant, the viscount found many elite Indian advocates of a country house aesthetic compatible with his own. The newly installed king of Avadh, he reported to his sister, 'has, besides his many palaces, five or six country houses, quite English, with English furniture and pictures'.[38] Diplomatic encounters such as these entailed lavish celebrations in which Indian princes and the commander-in-chief exchanged elaborate, costly gifts. East India Company policy strictly prohibited the retention of these presents by British officers,[39] but the printed memoirs published by Combermere's family and friends in the Victorian era clearly documented the flow of gifted Indian weaponry from these diplomatic encounters to Combermere

[34] These collecting practices are detailed in the first three lectures of this series: Margot Finn, 'Material Turns in British History: I. Loot', *Transactions of the Royal Historical Society*, 28 (2018), 5–32; *idem*, 'Material Turns in British History: II. Corruption: Imperial Power, Princely Power, Princely Politics and Gifts Gone Rogue', *Transactions of the Royal Historical Society*, 29 (2019), 1–25; and *idem*, 'Material Turns in British History: III. Collecting: Colonial Bombay, Basra, Baghdad and the Enlightenment Museum', *Transactions of the Royal Historical Society*, 30 (2020), 1–28.
[35] Combermere to Lord Amherst, 19 December 1825, 22 January 1826 and 24 January 1826, British Library, MSS Eur F140/80 (a).
[36] *Memoirs and Correspondence*, II, 126.
[37] *Ibid.*, II, 127. See also II, 215–16, 235–40.
[38] *Ibid.*, II, 159.
[39] See Finn, 'Material Turns: II. Corruption'.

Abbey.[40] The raja of Patiala, a connoisseur of both Indian and English material culture, gifted the commander-in-chief 'a complete suit of chain-armour ... inlaid with gold, a sword and shield, a bow and arrows, and a dagger', the viscount's Victorian biographers noted. 'These may now be seen in the armoury at Combermere, side by side with many other weapons obtained during his residence in India,' they observed.[41] Policy Exchange's 'History Matters' project identifies historians who draw attention to English material culture's imbrication with empire as a 'woke' cavalry intent on distorting national history by 'rewriting' it. Taking a longer view, however, of EIC material culture, it is the twentieth and twenty-first centuries' erasure of these colonial connections that is most striking, rather than historians' more recent attention to them. Already in the nineteenth century, Viscount Combermere's family and friends – no woke snowflakes they – drew repeated attention to the material legacies that flowed to Cheshire from India during his imperial career. There is no need to fall prey to the error against which Policy Exchange warns us – that is, 'judging our past with today's values'[42] – to acknowledge a fact self-evident to the Victorians. Empire and the violence upon which it was founded were bedrocks of the modern British nation state, providing the men who governed it with wealth, status and power that took conspicuous physical form in their stately homes.

Combermere Abbey's hybrid East (and West) Indian material culture is hardly anomalous. In September 2020, the National Trust published a report which identified ninety-three properties in its care in England and Wales with links to colonialism, including twenty-nine whose proprietors (like Combermere) received financial compensation for Parliament's abolition of slavery in 1834.[43] Ruffling many feathers, this important report amplified research on a much wider population of stately homes already in the public domain. In 2014, for example, historian Stephanie Barczewski identified hundreds of landed estates and country houses acquired with imperial wealth from 1700 to 1930. Of these, 229 were purchased or restored with East Indian fortunes between 1700 and 1850. The heyday of East India Company men's

---

[40] *Memoirs and Correspondence*, II, 171–2. See also II, 151–2, 159. This gifting is a frequent theme in the memoir of Combermere's aide-de-camp, Major Archer, *Tours in Upper India, and in Parts of the Himalaya Mountains; With an Account of the Courts of the Native Princes, &c.* (2 vols., 1833), for example I, 7–10, 188–9.

[41] *Memoirs and Correspondence*, II, 171–2.

[42] 'Policy Exchange launches new history project' (28 June 2020), https://policyexchange.org.uk/press-release/policy-exchange-launches-new-history-project.

[43] Sally-Anne Huxtable, Corinne Fowler, Christo Kefalas and Emma Slocombe (eds.), *Interim Report on the Connections between Colonialism and Properties in the Care of the National Trust, Including Links with Historic Slavery* (Swindon, 2020).

stately home acquisition extended from the 1760s to the 1810s.[44] Counties such as Angus, Berkshire, Hertfordshire and Perthshire featured especially prominently in this architectural feeding frenzy, but stately homes built with East India Company fortunes punctuated the landscape across the full range of British counties in these years.[45]

To be sure, not all Georgians and Victorians were as willing as Viscount Combermere to draw attention to the South Asian wellsprings of their country house lifestyles. In the stately homes of men from mercantile backgrounds who aspired to gentility and of members of the lesser gentry whose economic precarity threatened their status, a more self-conscious marriage between Indian wealth and material culture emerged.[46] These men's architectural preferences, artistic tastes and furnishing choices point us to a pervasive strand of imperial amnesia mediated by their stately homes – structures that were both made possible by colonial lives and used to mask the traces of empire in the families they funded and maintained.

The desire to preserve, repurchase or acquire a country house as a family seat repeatedly recurs in the biographies of the leading men who drove East India Company policies both on the subcontinent and in Parliament. The *Oxford Dictionary of National Biography* entry for Robert Clive notes that, born into a venerable but impecunious gentry family, 'Clive experienced a … peripatetic childhood and … spent much time away from his parents' and their Shropshire country house. On his first return from the subcontinent in 1753, Clive unsurprisingly used his Indian fortune of £40,000 to pay his family's debts, including the mortgage on the family seat. Together with the purchase of new landed estates, this country house base allowed him to enter Parliament and build an East India Company interest in the House of Commons.[47] Likewise, Warren Hastings used the savings garnered from his Indian career to recuperate the estate in Worcestershire to which his family traced its history continuously from the twelfth century. Returning to England in 1785, Hastings 'immediately set about trying to realize the objective that he had long set himself, the

---

[44] Stephanie Barczewski, *Country Houses and the British Empire, 1700–1930* (Manchester, 2014), esp. 52–3.

[45] This phenomenon is detailed in Margot Finn and Kate Smith (eds.), *The East India Company at Home, 1757–1857* (2018), available open access from www.uclpress.co.uk/products/88277.

[46] For the negative stereotypes associated with EIC men of wealth and their landed estates, see J. M. Holzman, *The Nabobs of England 1760–1815: A Study of the Returned Anglo-Indian* (New York, 1926) and Tillman Nechtman, *Nabobs: Empire and Identity in Eighteenth-Century Britain* (Cambridge, 2010).

[47] H. V. Bowen, 'Clive, Robert, first Baron Clive of Plassey (1725–1774)', *Oxford Dictionary of National Biography* (Oxford, 2004; 3 January 2008 version).

recovery of the Daylesford estate for the Hastings family', P. J. Marshall observes in the *Oxford Dictionary of National Biography*. Commissioning a new family seat by Samuel Pepys Cockerell, Hastings spent £60,000 of his £220,000 Indian fortune on Daylesford and its pleasure grounds, which he occupied with his wife from 1791, living 'the life of a country gentleman, engaged in local affairs and farming'.[48]

If we examine the external signifiers of East India Company men's country houses, processes of imperial erasure – Georgian-era architectural 'cancel culture', if you will – become conspicuously evident. Samuel Pepys Cockerell's most famous 'English' country house is not his reconstruction of Warren Hastings's beloved Daylesford, but instead the nearby, new home he designed for his own elder brother Charles in 1805. Charles (later Sir Charles) Cockerell retired from the East India Company civil service as a wealthy 'nabob' in 1801. He was typical of a late Georgian generation of Company men enriched far beyond their mercantile origins and determined to translate their prodigious Indian wealth into social and political power at home, through family seats set on landed estates and parliamentary seats at Westminster.[49] The entrance of these men into the House of Commons stoked fears of an 'Oriental' overthrow of British liberties; Cockerell indeed first sat for a notoriously corrupt Cornwall constituency that was in the gift of his 'fellow nabob', Richard Barwell.[50] But his country seat, fashioned in a pastiche of Indian architectural styles now termed neo-Mughal or Indo-Saracenic, is entirely atypical of East India Company country houses. Sezincote House reputedly inspired the Prince of Wales's construction of the Royal Pavilion at Brighton, but it failed to capture the imagination of East India Company men.[51] Their characteristic architectural aesthetic spanned from the monastic abbey to mock-Gothic structures, but was firmly centred in Palladianism and its neoclassical offshoots. These dominant styles rejected Indian influences, adopting instead 'the forms and ornament of ancient Roman buildings to create an architecture based on

[48] P. J. Marshall, 'Hastings, Warren (1732–1818)', *Oxford Dictionary of National Biography* (Oxford, 2004; 4 October 2008 version).

[49] J. W. Anderson and R. G. Thorne, 'Cockerell, Charles (1755–1837), of Sezincote, Glos.', in *The History of Parliament: The House of Commons 1790–1820*, ed. R. Thorne (Cambridge, 1986), www.historyofparliamentonline.org/volume/1790-1820/member/cockerell-charles-1755-1837.

[50] Philip Lawson and Jim Phillips, '"Our execrable banditti": Perceptions of Nabobs in Mid-eighteenth Century Britain', *Albion*, 16 (1984), 225–41; Anderson and Thorne, 'Cockerell'.

[51] Christopher Edward Clive Hussey, 'Sezincote, Gloucestershire', *Country Life*, 85 (1939), 502–6, 528–32; Jan Sibthorpe and Ellen Filor, 'Outside the Public: The Histories of Sezincote and Prestonfield in Private Hands', in *New Paths to Public Histories*, ed. Margot Finn and Kate Smith (Basingstoke, 2015), 100–135.

symmetry, proportion and perspective'.[52] Sir Francis Sykes's new country house at Basildon Park in Berkshire and Sir Thomas Rumbold's new house at Woodhall Park in Hertfordshire exemplify this trend.[53] In Wales, William Paxton's neoclassical new-build, Middleton Hall, likewise emphatically announced that this erstwhile East India Company surgeon had arrived in the gentry.[54] North of the border, Novar House no less triumphantly signalled the return of Sir Hector Munro to his ancestral lands with the spoils of Indian warfare, which allowed him dramatically to expand his family home, reconfiguring its footprint as a classical square.[55]

'Nabob' was a term of abuse in Georgian Britain. A Persian word that designated a provincial governor in the Mughal empire, 'nawab' was transmogrified into nabob by vociferous British critics of the East India Company's nascent empire in the aftermath of Clive's victory at Plassey. To contemporaries, nabobism signified all that was wrong with East India Company rule: famine and exploitation on the subcontinent, followed by an inflow of excessive new wealth and political corruption to Britain – both signified by the purchase and extravagant refashioning of rural stately homes.[56] 'Here is a specimen of the new ... aristocracy created ... against the natural interests of this kingdom,' Edmund Burke declaimed in the House of Commons in 1785, excoriating the nabob Paul Benfield. 'A ... criminal, who long since ought to have fattened the region [sic] kites with his offal, is ... enfeoffed with an estate, which ... effaces the splendor [sic] of all the nobility of Europe,' Burke raged.[57] James Gillray's 1797 caricature of Benfield, riding in front of his Palladian country house in Hertfordshire, registered the perceived dangers to the polity of this Asian wealth by racialising Benfield as 'black'.[58]

[52] 'Palladianism', www.vam.ac.uk/collections/palladianism.

[53] See the National Trust's 'History of Basildon Park', www.nationaltrust.org.uk/basildon-park/features/history-of-basildon-park; and Historic Houses' 'Woodhall Park', www.historic-houses.org/house/woodhall-park/visit/.

[54] W. G. J. Kuiters, 'Paxton, Sir William (1743/4–1824)', *Oxford Dictionary of National Biography* (Oxford, 2004); Lowri Ann Rees, 'Welsh Sojourners in India: The East India Company, Networks and Patronage, c. 1760–1840', *Journal of Imperial and Commonwealth History*, 45 (2017), 165–87, at 167. Significantly, Paxton's neoclassical Middleton Hall was designed for him by Samuel Pepys Cockerell.

[55] Andrew Mackillop, 'The Highlands and the Returning Nabob: Sir Hector Munro of Novar, 1760–1807', in *Emigrant Homecomings: The Return Movement of Emigrants, 1600–2000*, ed. Marjory Harper (Manchester, 2005), 233–61.

[56] Nechtman, *Nabobs*, offers the most comprehensive analysis of this phenomenon.

[57] Edmund Burke, 'Speech on the Nabob of Arcot's Debts', in *The Writings and Speeches of Edmund Burke: Volume V. India: Madras and Bengal 1774–1785*, ed. P. J. Marshall (Oxford, 1981), 544–5.

[58] See James Gillray, 'Count Rupee', published by Hannah Humphrey 5 June 1797, National Portrait Gallery, NPG D12616: www.npg.org.uk/collections/search/person/mp61740/paul-benfield.

In this fraught political context, not least among the virtues of neoclassical and neo-Gothic country house facades was their role in downplaying the South Asian origins of Company men's wealth and power. Inside stately homes, Georgian and early Victorian propertied elites navigated uneasily between the celebration, the domestication and the denial of the Indian taproots of their British fortunes. Armorial porcelain crafted in Jingdezhen and elaborate Chinese wallpaper were luxury furnishings to which families with East India Company connections enjoyed disproportionate access.59 Highly prized by members of the Georgian governing elite, today they are carefully preserved in the collections of the National Trust, providing a visual record of patterns of imperialism whose virtues have been hotly contested in Britain since the eighteenth century.60 Women participated avidly in the imperial collecting practices that shaped this material culture. In South India, while her husband, the governor of Madras Presidency, worked to install a new, Hindu princely government after the defeat of Tipu Sultan in 1799, Lady Henrietta Clive, travelled extensively throughout Mysore. Accompanied by her teenage daughters, she collected loot, booty and luxury merchandise for Powis Castle, the family seat in Wales. Here the ornate chintz tent that had earlier accompanied Tipu Sultan on travels to survey his domains offered an arresting visual reminder of his defeat, when put to domestic use at Lady Clive's elite garden parties.61

In Georgian portraiture, we find intriguing material traces of the black lives that mattered to the elite status of this imperial ruling class.62 Many South Asian domestic workers accompanied East India Company families from the subcontinent to stately homes in Britain, both as servants and as enslaved domestic staff.63 Sir Hector Munro returned home to Scotland from his Indian campaigns with an entourage that included 'a BLACK SLAVE, a native of the East Indies, called CÆSAR', who, having absconded from his master's country house in 1771, was

---

59 Finn and Smith (eds.), *East India Company at Home.*

60 Huxtable *et al., Interim Report.*

61 Nancy K. Shields (ed.), *Birds of Passage: Henrietta Clive's Travels in South India 1798–1801* (2009).

62 See for example the portrait of Sir Hector Munro and his Indian manservant, attributed to David Martin and painted in 1785 after Munro's return to Scotland from the subcontinent: National Portrait Gallery, London, NPG 1433, www.npg.org.uk/collections/search/portrait/mwo4577/Sir-Hector-Munro.

63 Satyasikha Chakraborty, '"Nurses of Our Ocean Highways": The Precarious Metropolitan Lives of Colonial South Asian Ayahs', *Journal of Women's History*, 32 (2020), 37–64; Michael Fisher, 'Bound for Britain: Changing Conditions of Servitude, 1600–1857', in *Slavery & South Asian History*, ed. Indrani Chatterjee and Richard Eaton (Bloomington, IN, 2006), 187–209.

advertised for in the *Caledonian Mercury*.[64] In the early nineteenth century, having retired to Berkshire from Bengal, William Hickey was attended by, and painted with, his Indian manservant, William Munnoo. Their joint portrait, exhibited at the Royal Academy in 1820, designated William Munnoo as 'black', reminding us of the extended timeline and complex composition of black British histories.[65] Hickey's social circle in Bengal had included the family of Sir Henry Russell. In England, he resumed his friendship with Lady Russell, who had returned home with her youngest, Indian-born children and two Indian servants while her husband and eldest sons remained in India, accumulating the capital with which, in 1820, they would purchase a stately home.[66] As Lady Russell tested country house life in Surrey, Kent and Somerset, she was accompanied and supported by Indian attendants. 'I have found both my Black Women faithful good Souls ... As to Anne Ayah she has really so attached herself to me that I think I never can part with her,' Lady Russell wrote in 1805. 'Anne Ayah (who is now call'd Mrs Williams, being my Maid) I cannot part with, she is in many respects superior to an English Servant, and in no one inferior – her attachment to me is quite wonderful,' she enthused a year later.[67]

## III  The selective, collective amnesias of imperial imagination

The Berkshire country house Lady Russell's husband and eldest son acquired in 1820, Swallowfield Park, embodies in its history, fabric and furnishings many of the contradictions, silences and erasures that marked (and masked) East India Company material culture. Its exterior gives no sign of Swallowfield's extended connection with empire in the East and West Indies.[68] But the Russells' extensive family archive sheds light on its many vestiges of empire – some obscured, but others displayed in plain view. Henry Russell, whose father Sir Henry Russell

---

[64] *Caledonian Mercury*, 22 June 1771. Further examples of Indian (as well as African and Caribbean) enslaved runaways in Britain can be identified from the Runaway Slaves in Britain: Bondage, Freedom and Race in the Eighteenth Century database: www.runaways. gla.ac.uk.

[65] See the 1819 portrait by William Thomas of William Hickey of the EIC civil service, depicted at home in England with his Indian manservant, William Munnew (or Munnoo), National Portrait Gallery, London, NPG 3249, www.npg.org.uk/collections/ search/portrait/mw03129/William-Munnew-or-Munnoo-William-Hickey. For William Munnew's legal status, see Fisher, 'Bound for Britain', 203–5.

[66] Margot Finn, 'Swallowfield Park, Berkshire: From Royalist Bastion to Empire Home', in *East India Company at Home*, eds, Finn and Smith, 205–30, 461–6.

[67] Lady Russell to Charles Russell, 12 March 1805 and 30 March 1806, Bodleian Library, MS Eng. Lett. c. 154, ff. 66v. and 101.

[68] Lady Constance Russell, *Swallowfield and Its Owners* (1901) provides both images of the house and perspectives on its history from the Tudors to the Victorian era.

had served as chief justice in Bengal, amassed a substantial collection of Indian art while serving as the Company's diplomatic representative at Hyderabad.[69] At Swallowfield, this artwork, a portrait of Russell by Romney and copies of paintings by old masters he acquired with his Indian savings together adorned the walls. Keen to consolidate and burnish his family's lineage, the second baronet carefully constructed a gallery of family portraits, commissioning the society artist David Wilkie to retouch a painting of his paternal grandmother, to make her more genteel.[70]

Excluded from Swallowfield's family gallery, however, was Henry's mixed-race daughter, Mary Wilson, one of three children born to him and his several Indian concubines. Sent 'home' to Britain on a separate ship to her father, his wife and their legitimate, white children, Mary was established at a boarding school in Clapham and trained up to be a governess, under the guardianship of Major Pitman, a retired East India Company military officer who had served at Hyderabad with her father. Despatched as an adolescent to service in a Devonshire country house, Mary Wilson repeatedly begged her guardian to know whose child she was. Her father was insistent both that his identity be kept from her, and that she should not set foot in his Berkshire country house.[71] Material legacies of empire were clearly one thing to display, human legacies quite another.

There is no need, anachronistically, to apply twenty-first-century sensibilities to censure Henry Russell's treatment of his mixed-heritage daughter. Her guardian, Major Pitman, as well as Henry's brothers and in-laws were both bemused and infuriated by his intransigence on this score. '[T]he dear childs [sic] mind for some time back has been much agitated on the subject of her birth, of which I have avoided giving her any explanation,' Major Pitman wrote to Sir Henry in 1838. 'At her age it is natural she should think deeply on a subject so interesting to her and I hope … you will agree with me in … setting her mind at rest regarding it,' he pleaded.[72] Russell's brothers, his wife's sister and his brother-in-law all happily met and acknowledged Mary Wilson, commenting openly on her physical resemblance to her father. But Russell, citing the interests of his wife and legitimate, white daughters to justify his reasoning, repeatedly refused to declare his paternity. 'For the

---

[69] Examples include a watercolour of the emperor Akbar watching an elephant fight, painted *c.* 1780 and purchased by Russell in Hyderabad *c.* 1800–20, now in the National Gallery of Australia, accession no. 91.1409: https://searchthecollection.nga.gov.au/object?uniqueId=157166.

[70] Finn, 'Swallowfield Park', 223–4.

[71] *Ibid.*, 229–30.

[72] Major Pitman to Sir Henry Russell, 2nd Bt, 14 April 1838, Bodleian Library, MS Eng. Lett. c. 170, f. 26.

present I am satisfied ... that we cannot tell Mary, whose daughter she is,' he wrote to Pitman in 1839.

> In the first place, I could not tell her who she is, without at the same time receiving her at least occasionally into my house, and I find, what is perhaps not only natural but proper, that Lady R. would object to this, at all counts while her own daughters are unmarried.[73]

Tracking the Indian capital inherited by Henry Russell's sisters – Mary Wilson's aunts – also leads us to English country houses. Like Swallowfield, at first glance the stately homes they inhabited in Lancashire and Devon appear to be quintessentially English. The drawing room of Henrietta Greene née Russell's country house was filled with fine furniture crafted locally by Gillows of Lancaster.[74] But the house itself, Whittington Hall, was a new build financed in no small part with capital from Henrietta's dowry, funded by savings from her father's salary as a judge on the Calcutta Supreme Court.[75] The neoclassical exterior of Winslade Park, the country house in Devon in which Henry's sister Rose resided, likewise simultaneously reflected and concealed imperial fortunes. Constructed earlier in the century for the nabob Edward Cotsford, Winslade had been purchased by Rose Porter née Russell's father-in-law, who was the proprietor of substantial estates in British Guiana. Rose's dowry provided an injection of Indian capital into the Porter finances when she married into the family in 1820. Abolition in 1834 brought the couple a second financial windfall. As the proprietor of 709 enslaved humans, Porter received £35,960 in compensation from Parliament, just under £2.5 million in today's money.[76]

At multiple levels and across the generations, country house material culture played vital roles in effacing the imperial past from contemporaries' memory. This selective amnesia was neither a passive nor an

---

[73] Sir Henry Russell to Major Pitman, 9 October 1839, Bodleian Library, MS Eng. Lett. c. 170, f. 51.

[74] Richard T. Lonsdale's painting of the interior of 'The Drawing Room at Whittington Hall, Lancashire', commissioned c. 1836 by Henrietta's husband, the MP Thomas Greene, depicts a cosy, English domestic interior 'splendidly furnished by the well-known cabinet-making firm of Gillows of Lancaster', as the Art Fund's notes observe: www.artfund.org/supporting-museums/art-weve-helped-buy/artwork/7086/the-drawing-room-at-whittington-hall-lancashire. Conventionally viewed as quintessentially 'English', Gillows's business enterprise was, in fact, closely imbricated with Caribbean slavery from the 1770s onward. See K. E. Ingram, 'The West Indian Trade of an English Furniture Firm', *Jamaican Historical Review*, 3 (1962), 22–37.

[75] For Thomas Greene, see Margaret Escott, 'Greene, Thomas (1794–1872), of Slyne and Whittington Hall, Lancs', in *The History of Parliament: The House of Commons 1820–1832*, ed. D. R. Fisher (Cambridge, 2009), www.historyofparliamentonline.org/volume/1820-1832/member/greene-thomas-1794-1872.

[76] Legacies of British Slave-ownership database, www.ucl.ac.uk/lbs/person/view/8022. See also https://historicengland.org.uk/listing/the-list/list-entry/1097566.

innocent process. We can trace its lineaments alike in stately home construction, in the decorative arts that defined a new Georgian country
house aesthetic and in Victorian family-history writing. The biography
of a silver-gilt presentation vase at Swallowfield brings this process of
imperial erasure into clear view. In 1901, Swallowfield's then chatelaine,
Lady Constance Russell, published a biography of her marital home,
rooting its place in history firmly in the Tudor era and underlining its historic ties to the British monarchy.[77] A commemorative vase dating from
1823 was one of the very few Russell family ties to India she chose to
acknowledge. Funded by a subscription of over £1,000 presented to
Henry Russell on his departure from Hyderabad in 1820, this decorative
object, Lady Russell proudly proclaimed, was a small token of his colleagues' appreciation for Russell's imperial service. The records in the
East India Company archive tell a very different story. In 1818, two
years before his precipitate departure from Hyderabad, Russell had
taken the law into his own hands, stepping beyond his diplomatic authority to order the flogging of two Indian men implicated in a robbery in the
city's bazaar. He subjected each man to 1,000 lashes, a punishment
administered by his brother-in-law. Within two days, both prisoners
were dead.[78] The Company's military officers at Hyderabad swiftly
mobilised in defence of this brutal flogging, but the governor general
and Council in Calcutta were outraged at Russell's actions, and he
resigned his post before he could be sacked. The vase, a 'Tribute of
Grateful Remembrance' funded by his subordinates at Hyderabad,
was commissioned in the aftermath of this disgrace and proudly displayed at Swallowfield.[79] Unsurprisingly, when it was auctioned in
Salisbury in 2010, it was Lady Russell's patriotic version of its proven-
ance, not the archival record of its contested heritage, that the auction-
eers cited in their catalogue.[80]

## IV Conclusions

Today contested heritage figures prominently in a so-called culture war
that rages across parliamentary politics, heritage organisations, educational institutions and social media. The secretary of state for culture
has warned ostensibly arm's-length heritage organisations that they
risk their funding if they 'politicise' history, while the minister for

[77] Russell, *Swallowfield*.
[78] Finn, 'Swallowfield Park', 226–8.
[79] *Ibid.*
[80] Accompanied by an extensive quotation from Lady Russell's book to secure its prov-
enance, the vase was estimated at £20,000–30,000 by Wooley & Wallis and purchased by
London dealers Koopman Rare Art for £95,000: www.antiquestradegazette.com/news/
2010/london-dealers-bid-95-000-for-rundell-vase-in-salisbury.

equalities has charged any schoolteacher who uncritically deploys Critical Race Theory with 'breaking the law'.[81] On Twitter and in the pages of the *Daily Mail*, the *Telegraph* and *The Times*, these sentiments have found a warm reception, as indignant readers have declaimed against 'cancel culture' even as they have ostentatiously withdrawn their support from charities such as the National Trust by destroying their membership cards and cancelling their subscriptions.[82]

In this lecture, I have used the entwined material histories of the East India Company and the British country house to question two fundamental premises of our twenty-first-century culture wars. First, my reading of the imperial histories of stately homes since the eighteenth century challenges the claim, made by projects such as Policy Exchange's 'History Matters', that present-day critiques of Britain's imperial past represent a novel, present-minded, 'woke' challenge to Britons' shared conception of the nation and its history. Rather, by pointing to Georgian-era diatribes against East India Company 'nabobs', I have suggested that such critiques were fundamental to many eighteenth- and nineteenth-century men and women's understanding of their own times. In the fabric, the artwork and the decorative cultures of the country houses they inhabited, we can trace a much earlier, highly politicised genealogy of heritage contests which continues to animate public understanding of the past today. By the Victorian era, Palladian and neo-Gothic architecture had definitively triumphed over the neo-Mughal, Indo-Saracenic style championed by Samuel Pepys Cockerell. By attending to the longer histories of British attitudes to empire, we can begin to understand why. For the frequent assertion that critiques of imperialism today anachronistically subject past generations to twenty-first-century belief systems itself effaces from the historical record men, women and children who challenged slavery, racial bias and imperial conquest decades (and indeed centuries) ago. Their histories too can be found in the archives and in the artistic legacies of the country house, if we choose to seek them, rather than complacently, unthinkingly asserting that our moral values today invariably trump those of the generations that preceded us.

Second, my interpretation questions the commonplace claim that by rewriting familiar narratives of national icons such as country houses, historians fundamentally distort the settled verities of a stable past. Instead, I have suggested that rewriting history was an essential function of the country house, and that Georgian and Victorian families residing

---

[81] Above, footnotes 10 and 11.

[82] Dominic Sandbrook's 'How dare the National Trust link Wordsworth to slavery because his brother sailed a ship to China?', *Daily Mail*, 23 September 2020, exemplifies the dominant tone and substance of this critique.

in stately homes were fully alive to this political purpose. The selective acquisition of desirable imperial luxuries, the selective exclusion of mixed-race progeny and the selective rewriting of family members' records of colonial service are all conspicuous in the amnesiac archives of Britons' stately homes.[83] Nor is recognition of the integral role of selective remembering and forgetting in shaping nations a modish, politically correct development of our century. Rather, it has been an axiom of historical analysis since at least the Victorian period. Ernest Renan, who was a close friend and intellectual companion of Sir Mountstuart Grant Duff – the fourth president of the Royal Historical Society, a former governor of Madras and no woke snowflake – articulated this argument forcefully in *Qu'est-ce qu'une nation?* (*What is a Nation?*), published in 1882:

> Forgetting, I would even say historical error, is an essential factor in the creation of a nation and it is for this reason that the progress of historical studies often poses a threat to nationality. Historical inquiry, in effect, throws light on the violent acts that have taken place at the origin of every political formation, even those that have been the most benevolent in their consequences. Unity is always brutally established.[84]

Bitterly contested at the time of its rapid territorial expansion in the aftermath of Clive's victory at Plassey, the East India Company played an instrumental role in forging the modern British state. Beyond passing mentions of Clive's statue at Whitehall, however, references to Britain's extended imperial history in South Asia are thin on the ground in the culture wars of the twenty-first century. This absence speaks eloquently to the ease with which we all fall prey to historical amnesia, and to the success with which earlier generations campaigned in and through their stately homes to encourage us to do so.

It is not the historian's role to serve as the handmaiden of public opinion by amplifying that pervasive, carefully constructed, selective view of the past – a view that is itself merely the most recent iteration of a long succession of interested forgettings and rememberings. Rather, rewriting history is precisely what historians do; it is how history works. There is no need to enter the lists of a novel culture war to rewrite the history of Britain's imperial past. That pathway is already well trodden, thanks to our Georgian and Victorian forebears.

---

[83] Finn, 'Swallowfield Park'. For broader discussions of these processes of erasure, see for example Catherine Hall, Keith McClelland, Nick Draper, Kate Donington and Rachel Lang, *Legacies of British Slave-ownership: Colonial Slavery and the Formation of Victorian Britain* (Cambridge, 2014), ch. 5 and Katie Donington, *The Bonds of Family: Slavery, Commerce and Culture in the British Atlantic World* (Manchester, 2019).

[84] Ernest Renan, *Qu'est-ce qu'une nation?*, trans. Ethan Rundell as *What Is a Nation?* (Paris, 1992), 3. For Grant Duff and Renan, see Sir Mountstuart E. Grant Duff, *Ernest Renan: In Memoriam* (1893). Grant Duff's 'liberal' vision of history is discussed in the first lecture in this series, Finn, 'Material Turns I: Loot', 28–31.

*Transactions of the RHS* 31 (2021), pp. 23–47 © The Author(s), 2021. Published by Cambridge University Press on behalf of the Royal Historical Society. This is an Open Access article, distributed under the terms of the Creative Commons Attribution licence (https://creative commons.org/licenses/by/4.0/), which permits unrestricted re-use, distribution, and reproduction in any medium, provided the original work is properly cited.
doi:10.1017/S0080440121000025

# RESPONDING TO VIOLENCE: LITURGY, AUTHORITY AND SACRED PLACES, *c.* 900–*c.* 1150

## By Sarah Hamilton

READ 1 MAY 2020

ABSTRACT. The principle that church buildings constitute sacred spaces, set apart from the secular world and its laws, is one of the most enduring legacies of medieval Christianity in the present day. When and how church buildings came to be defined as sacred has consequently received a good deal of attention from modern scholars. What happened when that status was compromised, and ecclesiastical spaces were polluted by acts of violence, like the murder of Archbishop Thomas Becket in Canterbury Cathedral? This paper investigates the history of rites for the reconciliation of holy places violated by the shedding of blood, homicide or other public acts of 'filthiness' which followed instances such as Becket's murder. I first identify the late tenth and early eleventh centuries in England as crucial to the development of this rite, before asking why English bishops began to pay attention to rites of reconciliation in the years around 1000 CE. This paper thus offers a fresh perspective on current understandings of ecclesiastical responses to violence in these years, the history of which has long been dominated by monastic evidence from west Frankia and Flanders. At the same time, it reveals the potential of liturgical rites to offer new insights into medieval society.

The murder of the Archbishop of Canterbury, Thomas Becket, in his own cathedral on 29 December 1170 led to the closure of that church, and the suspension of all liturgical services there for almost a year.[1] Services only resumed some 357 days later on 21 December 1171, because the building itself needed to be ritually cleansed and restored from the violence which had occurred inside.[2] It took so long to

---

[1] The most comprehensive modern account of Becket's life and death remains that of Frank Barlow, *Thomas Becket*, 3rd edn (1997).

[2] The 'Landsdowne Anonymous': 'in die tertia ante natale Domini ecclesiam Cantuariensem reconciliaverunt, et officia sua celebrare apostolica auctoritate monachis eiusdem ecclesiae indulserunt.' *Materials for the History of Thomas Becket, Archbishop of Canterbury*, ed. J. C. Robertson and J. B. Sheppard, Rolls Series 67 (7 vols., 1875–85) (hereinafter *MHTB*), IV, 169. The cathedral's crypt, the site of Becket's tomb, had been opened to the crowds of pilgrims already flocking to the site some nine months earlier around Easter (4 April 1171): Benedict of Peterborough, *Miraculae S. Thomae Cantuariensis*, 2.6, *MHTB*, II, 60;

reopen the church because advice about what to do in such circumstances was sought from the pope. The letter Alexander III (1159–81) wrote to his two legates on the subject is worth quoting:

> We entrust to you how you are to reconcile the church of Canterbury: thus the sacrament of the original dedication ought not to be repeated, but just as it is the custom to do in the church of blessed Peter, blessed water should be splashed about.[3]

The papal legates consequently wrote to the prior and the community of Christ Church which served the cathedral, instructing them to call the abbots and bishops of their province to a solemn assembly so that they could 'consecrate your church anew'.[4] In a service conducted by Bartholomew, Bishop of Exeter, and attended by all the leading churchmen of southern England, the cathedral was, in the words of one later chronicler, 'restored to its pristine state' on the feast of Becket's namesake, St Thomas the Apostle.[5]

Becket's murder was shocking; it was also highly unusual.[6] The texts cited above were all written close to the event and give the impression that what took place on 21 December 1171 was an unusual, even innovative, rite; advice had to be sought from the pope, who prescribed that a rite be conducted as at St Peter's in Rome. This impression of novelty is strengthened by the variation in the vocabulary used by different contemporary writers to describe the reconciliation service. The author of the Landsdowne Anonymous's account of the aftermath of Becket's murder described how the assembled clergy 'reconciled the church of Canterbury (*reconciliaverunt*)'.[7] Reconciliation is also the term used by Pope Alexander III in his instructions (cited above) to his legates that

on Benedict's account and the timetable for the development of a cult around Becket see Rachel Koopmans, *Wonderful to Relate: Miracle Stories and Miracle Collecting in High Medieval England* (Philadelphia, 2011), 139–58, particularly 144–5.

[3] 'Mandamus vobis quatenus ecclesiam Cantuariae faciatis reconciliari, ita tamen ut sacramentum pristinae dedicationis non debeat iterari, sed, sicut solet fieri in ecclesia beati Petri, tantum aqua benedicta aspergatur. Bene valete.' No. 787, *MHTB*, VII, 551.

[4] 'convocatis episcopis et abbatibus provinciae vestrae qui vobis ad hoc idonei visi fuerint, cum solemnitate congrua, adhibito solemnitatis ecclesiasticae, sicut majoribus visum fuit, moderamine, denuo ecclesiam vestram consecretis.' No. 788, *MHTB*, VII, 552.

[5] 'sed tandem ad matris suae Dorobernensis ecclesiae vocationem in festo Sancti Thomae apostoli suffraganei convenerunt episcopi, ut ecclesiam, longa suspensione consternatam, juxta mandatum domini papae in statum pristinum reformarent.' Roger of Wendover, *Liber qui dicitur Flores Historiarum*, ed. H. G. Hewlett, Rolls Series (3 vols., 1886–9), I, 89. Roger's account of the years up to 1202 is based on an earlier text compiled probably at St Albans, which was itself based on earlier texts. This account is not to be found in any surviving earlier sources. For a helpful account of Roger see David Corner, 'Roger of Wendover (d.1236)', *Oxford Dictionary of National Biography Online*.

[6] Unusual but not unknown: on this phenomenon, and its chronological and geographical contours, across the medieval Latin West see the contributions in *Bischofsmord im Mittelalter. Murder of Bishops*, ed. Natalie Fryde and Dirk Reitz (Göttingen, 2003).

[7] 'The Landsdowne Anonymous', *MHTB*, IV, 169; see n. 2 above.

the Roman rite be followed. When it came time for them to pass these instructions on to the community of Christ Church, they chose instead to refer to the service not as a reconciliation but rather a chance to 'consecrate (the church) anew (*denuo ecclesiam vestram consecretis*)'.[8]

The legates' description of this rite as consecrating the cathedral 'anew' is reminiscent of contemporary debates in canon law about the circumstances in which a church might need to be reconsecrated. The influential twelfth-century compilation of canon law, Gratian's *Decretum*, included a canon that if the church has been violated, by either homicide or adultery, then it should be cleansed most diligently and consecrated anew.[9] Gratian's account provided the foundation for the late thirteenth-century interpretation of this reconciliation rite by William Durandus, the southern French bishop of Mende, in his treatise on the symbolism of divine offices. There Durandus argued that it was not necessary to reconcile the church after all forms of bloodshed, such as nosebleeds or menstruation, but only after acts of violence.[10] To date, scholarly considerations of this rite, to the extent they exist, have largely focused on the later Middle Ages. In fact, as this paper will suggest, there is good reason to suppose that the reconciliation service for holy sites polluted by violence was well known in England before Becket's murder, and indeed that the roots of this rite lie in the tenth century, if not earlier.[11] For a rite 'for the reconciliation of altars or sacred places or cemeteries where blood has been spilt or homicide

---

[8] No. 788, *MHTB*, VII, 551–2. See n. 4 above.

[9] ' Si homicidio uel adulterio ecclesia uiolata fuerit, diligentissime expurgetur et denuo consecretur.', *Decretum Gratiani*, c. 19, *de Cons*, d. I, *Corpus iuris canonici I: Decretum magistri Gratiani*, ed. E. Friedberg (Leipzig, 1879), digitised at https://geschichte.digitale-sammlungen.de//decretum-gratiani (last accessed 28 February 2021). On Gratian see Anders Winroth, *The Making of Gratian's* Decretum (Cambridge, 2000).

[10] William Durandus, *Rationale Divinorum Officiorum*, I.vi.40–6, ed. A. Davril and T. M. Thibodeau, Corpus Christianorum Continuatio Mediaevalis 140, 140A, 140B (Turnhout, 1995–2000), I, 80–4.

[11] William Maskell, *Monumenta Ritualia Ecclesiae Anglicanae. The Occasional Offices of the Church of England According to the Old Use of Salisbury, the Prymer in English and Other Prayers and Forms with Dissertations and Notes* (Oxford, 1882), cccxxxviii–cccxlvi; John Theophilus Gulczynski, *The Desecration and Violation of Churches: An Historical Synopsis and Commentary* (Washington, DC, 1942); Derek A. Rivard bases his account of the continental rites for reconciliation of violated churches on those edited by Michel Andrieu, beginning with the eleventh-century 'Romano-German' rite, in his study of the role of liturgical blessing in the lives of central medieval Christians, but does not investigate their origins: *Blessing the World: Ritual and Lay Piety in Medieval Religion* (Washington, DC, 2009), 112–30. The rites identified by Edmond Martène in the early eighteenth century remain fundamental to any student: *De Antiquis Ecclesiae Ritibus Libri*, ed. E. Martène (Antwerp, 4 vols., 1736; repr. Hildesheim, 1967), Lib. II, c. xv, II, 793–803. A.-G. Martimort's identification of the manuscripts edited by Martène reveals that his examples, where known, are all later tenth- and eleventh-century: *La documentation liturgique de Dom Edmond Martène* (Vatican City, 1978), 400–2.

taken place or some other public filthiness (or superstition) carried out' is already to be found in a bishop's service book associated with early twelfth-century Canterbury and now in Trinity College Dublin, which was probably made for Archbishop Anselm (1093–1109).[12] As this paper suggests, it is distinctly possible that that particular iteration of the rite was the basis for that used in Canterbury in 1171. Indeed, as will become clear, a rite for the reconciliation of violated holy places had already been a staple of southern English service books and church law for a century and a half before Anselm. All those involved in orchestrating the service after Becket's murder – the pope, his two legates, Bishop Bartholomew of Exeter, Prior Odo of Christ Church, Canterbury, and the assembled bishops and abbots – were already familiar with the rites for the reconciliation of those sacred places where blood has been spilt which are the subject of this paper.

The origins of this rite lie much earlier. Dedication rites to make a building into a church have deep roots in the early Church and were reserved to the bishop from the sixth century onwards, if not earlier.[13] Dedication rites made ecclesiastical spaces sacred and set apart from the secular world, and consequently they have been the subject of a good deal of recent attention. Scholars have identified the period from the ninth to the eleventh century as a crucial time for the development of the church building (and its surroundings) as a separate, sacred space in the Latin Christian West.[14] What has been much less noticed,

---

[12] 'In reconciliatione altaris uel sacri loci seu cymiterii ubi sanguis fuerit effusus aut homicidium factum aut aliqua spurcitia publice perpetrata.' Dublin, Trinity College, MS 98, ff. 29v–35r. For a description of this manuscript see M. L. Colker, *Trinity College Library Dublin: Descriptive Catalogue of the Mediaeval and Renaissance Latin Manuscripts* (Aldershot, 1991); for a digitised copy see Digital Collections, the Library of Trinity College Dublin: https://digitalcollections.tcd.ie/concern/works/d504rq89v?locale=en (last accessed 14 June 2021). For the argument that it was made for Archbishop Anselm in the late eleventh century, see Malcolm Gullick and Richard W. Pfaff, 'The Dublin Pontifical [TCD 98 [B.3.6]: St Anselm's?', *Scriptorium*, 55 (2001), 284–94, plates 58–60.

[13] *Synodus Bracarensis prima*, c. 18, *Edition der falschen Kapitularien des Benedictus Levita*, ed. G. Schmitz, http://www.benedictus.mgh.de/quellen/chga/chga_057t.htm (last accessed 23 June 2021); Thomas Kozachek, 'The Repertory of Chant for Dedicating Churches in the Middle Ages: Music, Liturgy, and Ritual' (Ph.D. thesis, Harvard University, 1995), 2. For further discussion of the sixth-century Gallic evidence for church dedications see Rob Meens, 'Reconciling Disturbed Sacred Space: The Ordo for "Reconciling an Altar Where a Murder Has Been Committed" in the *Sacramentary of Gellone* in Its Cultural Context', in *The Merovingian Kingdoms and the Mediterranean World: Revisiting the Sources*, ed. Stefan Esders, Yitzhak Hen, Pia Lucas and Tamar Rotman (2019), 103–12.

[14] Michel Lauwers, *Naissance du cimetière. Lieux sacrés et terre des morts dans l'Occident médiéval* (Paris, 2005); D. Iogna-Prat, *La Maison Dieu. Une histoire monumentale de l'Église au Moyen Âge* (Paris, 2006) and his 'Churches in the Landscape', in *The Cambridge History of Christianity: Early Medieval Christianities c. 600–c.1100*, ed. Thomas F. X. Noble and Julia M. H. Smith (Cambridge, 2008), 363–79; *Mises en scène et mémoires de la consécration de l'église dans l'occident*

however, is that the focus on developing a liturgy for making spaces holy was accompanied from at least the 790s by an interest in what to do if that space was violated by acts of violence.[15] Yet some of the earliest surviving liturgical evidence for church dedication prayers is to be found in the late eighth-century Frankish world in three sacramentaries which also include prayers to reconcile a holy space which has been violated by blood being spilt.[16]

At around the same time the term *ecclesia* underwent a change in meaning. In late antiquity the word denoted a community of the faithful, but in the central Middle Ages it came to denote a particular physical site, enclosed and set apart from the secular world.[17] Dominique Iogna-Prat found the origins of this spatial turn in the meaning of *ecclesia* in the writings of ninth-century Carolingian churchmen, arguing that the idea of the church as a separate, sacred space was first fully developed in this Frankish context; Miriam Czock has pushed this back into the eighth century.[18] At the same time, the definition of *ecclesia* was expanded beyond the building in which worship took place to include cemeteries, the priest's house and land.[19] This changed the understanding of church buildings so they became not just places reserved for worship, but also places set apart from the secular world, symbolising the community of

---

*médiéval*, ed. Didier Méhu (Turnhout, 2007); Helen Gittos, *Liturgy, Architecture, and Sacred Places in Anglo-Saxon England* (Oxford, 2013).

[15] On the eighth-century context for the earliest records of this rite see now Meens, 'Reconciling Disturbed Sacred Space'.

[16] *Liber Sacramentorum Gellonensis*, ed. A. Dumas and J. Deshusses, Corpus Christianorum Series Latina (hereinafter CCSL) 159 (Turnhout, 1981), 351–2, 360–4 (nos. 352, 356); *Liber Sacramentorum Augustodunensis*, ed. O. Heiming, CCSL 159B (Turnhout, 1989), 165–70 (nos. 340–2); *Liber Sacramentorum Engolismensis*, ed. P. Saint-Roch, CCSL 159C (Turnhout, 1987), 301–5 (nos. 32–4). On the Gellone Sacramentary's evidence see Meens, 'Reconciling Disturbed Sacred Space'.

[17] Late antiquity witnessed the emergence of Christian ideas of holy place: Sabine MacCormack, 'Loca Sancta', in *Roman Religion*, ed. Clifford Ando (Edinburgh, 2003), 252–72 (originally published in *The Blessings of Pilgrimage*, ed. R. Ousterhout (Urbana, IL, 1990), 7–40); R. A. Markus, 'How on Earth Could Places Become Holy? Origins of the Christian Idea of Holy Places', *Journal of Early Christian Studies*, 2 (1994), 257–71.

[18] Iogna-Prat, *La Maison Dieu*. For a wider investigation of written discourse on church buildings in late antiquity and the early Middle Ages and the emergence of the idea of the church building as a holy site in Carolingian Frankia see Miriam Czock, *Gottes Haus. Untersuchungen zur Kirche als heiligem Raum von der Spätantike bis ins Frühmittelalter* (Berlin, 2012).

[19] For example, Regino of Prüm in his early tenth-century collection of canon law, compiled for the archbishops of Trier and Mainz, included this question in his prescription as to how the bishop should conduct the visitation of a local church: 'Investigandum, si habeat ipsa ecclesia mansum habentem bonoaria duodecim praeter cimiterium et curtem, ubi ecclesia et domus presbyteri continetur et si habeat mancipia quatuor?' (Investigate if his church has a courtyard of 12 *bonoaria* [measure of land roughly equivalent to a quarter of an acre] beside the cemetery and a courtyard in which the church and priest's house are contained and if he has 4 slaves'): *Libri Duo de Synodalibus Causis et Disciplinis Ecclesiasticis*, ed. F. G. A. Wasserschleben, rev. W. Hartmann (Darmstadt, 2004), I.1 (q. 14), 26.

the living and the dead but also offering a place of refuge from secular law.[20] This change was marked by the emergence in Frankia of liturgical rites for the consecration of churches from the seventh century, and their consolidation in the ninth century, and for the blessing of cemeteries in the tenth century.[21] These were liturgical responses to a fundamental change in the ecclesiastical geography of the Latin West: the increase in local churches.[22] Central to this development is the emergence and spread of parochial structures across the West, that is, the erection and maintenance of local churches funded by those living in the locality.[23] Alongside the proliferation in local church buildings came a shift in where the dead were buried. Between the seventh and twelfth centuries, the dead moved from their traditional Roman location outside the city walls to be situated next to the local church. Michel Lauwers termed this transformation *inecclesiamento* to capture the significance of this

---

[20] For a summary of medieval sanctuary's legal history see Karl Shoemaker, *Sanctuary and Crime in the European Middle Ages, 400–1500* (New York, 2010). Sanctuary's early medieval roots are complex, as revealed by Rob Meens, 'Sanctuary, Penance and Dispute Settlement under Charlemagne: The Conflict between Alcuin and Theodulf of Orléans over a Sinful Cleric,' *Speculum*, 82 (2007), 277–300.

[21] Gittos, *Liturgy*, 212–56; on Frankish rites see also Dana Polanichka, 'Transforming Space, (Per)forming Community: Church Consecration in Carolingian Europe', *Viator*, 43 (2012), 79–98. On rites for the consecration of cemeteries as an early tenth-century English development see Helen Gittos, 'Creating the Sacred: Anglo-Saxon Rites for Consecrating Cemeteries', in *Burial in Early Medieval England and Wales*, ed. Sam Lucy and Andrew Reynolds (2002), 195–208. Cécile Treffort has shown that there is no evidence for the consecration of cemeteries before the tenth century: 'Consécration de cimetière et contrôle épiscopal des lieux d'inhumation au Xe siècle', in *Le Sacré et son inscription dans l'espace à Byzance et en occident*, ed. Michel Kaplan (Paris, 2001), 285–99; she argues against Élisabeth Zadora-Rio's suggestion that this practice was only popularised in Francia in the late eleventh and twelfth centuries: 'Lieux d'inhumation et espaces consacrés: le voyage du pape Urbain II en France (août 1095–août 1096)', *Lieux sacrés, lieux de culte, sanctuaires*, ed. A. Vauchez, Collection de l'École française de Rome 273 (Rome, 2000), 197–213.

[22] Major works include M. Aubrun, *La paroisse en France. Des origines au XVe siècle* (Paris, 1986); John Blair, *The Church in Anglo-Saxon Society* (Oxford, 2005); Sarah Hamilton, *Church and People in the Medieval West, 900–1200* (Harlow, 2013), 31–59; Iogna-Prat, 'Churches in the Landscape', and *La Maison Dieu*; Maureen C. Miller, *The Formation of a Medieval Church: Ecclesiastical Change in Verona, 950–1150* (Ithaca, 1993); Susan Wood, *The Proprietary Church in the Medieval West* (Oxford, 2006), esp. part III. As these authors emphasise, this was a gradual process grounded in much earlier developments. For a summary of research on the early medieval period see *Men in the Middle: Local Priests in Early Medieval Europe*, ed. Steffen Patzold and Carine van Rhijn (Berlin, 2016), and now Paul Fouracre, *External Light and Earthly Concerns: Belief and the Shaping of Medieval Society* (Manchester, 2021).

[23] On tithes see J. Semmler, 'Zehntgebot und Pfarrtermination in karolingischer Zeit', in *Aus Kirche und Reich. Studien zu Theologies, Politik und Recht im Mittelalter. Festschrift für Friedrich Kempf*, ed. H. Mordek (Sigmaringen, 1983), 33–44; *La dîme, l'église et la société féodale*, ed. M. Lauwers (Turnhout, 2012); John Eldevik, *Episcopal Power and Ecclesiastical Reform in the German Empire: Tithes, Lordship, and Community, 950–1150* (Cambridge, 2012).

change in local landscapes.[24] Although the significance of the early medieval rite for the reconciliation of holy places has not been much noticed by modern researchers, either of Frankia or England, it has a good deal to tell us about how, when and why these changes came about.

In what follows I will start by investigating the evidence for the twelfth-century Canterbury rite available to Bishop Bartholomew of Exeter in 1171. I then consider how we should interpret this liturgical evidence by uncovering how the rite evolved between the time it was first recorded and the mid-twelfth century, with a focus on southern England. Tracing when and how this particular liturgical response to violent attacks on holy places came to be recorded in church law, I then ask how far these particular changes correspond with the developments in the liturgical record. In the final part, having established when and where the twelfth-century Canterbury rite first emerged, I will investigate the wider context in which it appeared, asking why this rite was recorded when it was, and what it reveals about the interaction of developments in ecclesiastical thought with wider social changes.

Quite which rite Bishop Bartholomew used to reconcile Canterbury Cathedral after Becket's murder cannot be known. The Magdalen Pontifical (Oxford, Magdalen College, Ms 226) is one of a group of pontifical manuscripts associated with Canterbury; it was copied in the mid-twelfth century and the rite it contains is therefore broadly proximate to the events of December 1171.[25] As the initial rubric makes clear, this rite assumes that the church building has previously been made holy through the rite of church dedication, but that that holiness has been contaminated by a violent act. It runs: '*On the reconciliation of the altars and holy places or cemeteries where blood has been spilt or homicide committed or other filthiness perpetrated publicly.*'[26] The rite in the Magdalen manuscript outlines the following stages:

- It begins with bishop, clergy and people processing in front of the church, singing an antiphon from Psalm 76, 'Thy way, O God, is in the holy place: who is the great God like our God', followed by two

[24] Lauwers, *Naissance du cimetière*, 269–76, quotation at p. 273.

[25] For dating the copying of this manuscript to the second quarter of the twelfth century as part of a group of manuscripts made at Canterbury see Helen Gittos, 'Sources for the Liturgy of Canterbury Cathedral in the Central Middle Ages', in *Medieval Art, Architecture and Archaeology at Canterbury*, ed. Alixe Bovey, Transactions of the British Archaeological Association 35 (2013), 21–58, at 53.

[26] *The Pontifical of Magdalen College*, ed. H. A. Wilson, Henry Bradshaw Society (hereinafter HBS) 39 (1910), 127–32 (hereinafter *PMC*): 'In reconciliatione altaris uel sacri loci seu cymiterii ubi sanguis fuerit effusus aut homicidium factum aut aliqua spurcitia puplice perpetrata', 127.

prayers requesting the Lord put demons to flight and purify the minds of those present.

- They then enter the church singing the antiphon 'Peace be in this house and on all its inhabitants', followed by prayer.
- The text specifies that the clergy should then recite the same 'litany as required in the dedication rite for an altar noted above'.[27]
- The bishop then makes the exorcism, blessing salt, ashes, water and wine as in the rite for the altar dedication, followed by a prayer requesting the reconciliation of this holy place or cemetery, and that it be consecrated or perpetually remain consecrated.[28] The aim is to avoid a repetition of the events which led up to this rite being performed.
- Afterwards the bishop processes around the church or cemetery three times inside and three times outside, sprinkling blessed water and singing another antiphon: 'Thou wilt sprinkle me, O Lord, with hyssop and I shall be cleansed.'[29] The prayers which follow request that the place be cleansed, restored and rebuilt: thus 'this place will be purged of all pollution, sanctified and restored to its prior state, and reconciled as sacred'.[30]
- The bishop then goes around the church inside and to the doors and to the cemetery with incense whilst singing an antiphon and Psalm 130, and requests that the church (or cemetery) (*hanc aecclesiam uel hoc cymiterium*) be sanctified as it had first been sanctified (echoes here of the legates' injunction to the cathedral community to consecrate the cathedral 'anew') and requests blessing and forgiveness of sins of both those who come to the oratory and those who are buried in the cemetery.[31]

---

[27] '*Postmodum faciat clerus letaniam quae supra notata est in dedicatione altaris.*' *PMC*, 128; compare that in the rite for the consecration of 'the house of the lord' (i.e. church, *not* altar), *ibid.*, 99–102. On the relationship of rites for consecration of the altar with those for the church see summary in Gittos, *Liturgy*, 215–19 and pp. 37–8 and 45 below.

[28] '*Deinde dicat episcopus ter Deus in adiutorium meum intende. Et faciat exorcismum et benedictionem salis cineris aquae et vini ut supra usque.* Quatinus consecrate sis aqua sancta ac proficias ad reconciliationem huius sacri loci uel cymiterii....uel hoc cymiterium diuinitus per gratiam spiritus sancti consecretur et perpetualiter ad inuocandum nomen domini conse-crata permaneat et spiritus sanctus habitet in hoc loco seu in hoc cimiterio.' *PMC*, 128.

[29] This antiphon is generally found in rites for the dedication of a church, consecration of a cemetery and that of a cross: *Cantus: A Database for Latin Ecclesiastical Chant: Inventories of Chant Sources* (cantus.uwaterloo.ca; last accessed 7 March 2021).

[30] 'Cuius maiestatem precamur ut hic locus fiat ab omni pollutione purgatus et sanctifi-catus atque in priorem statum restitutus et reconciliatus ac sacratus.'; see also 'Deus cuius bonitas nec principium nec finem habet cuius est polluta purgare neglecta restaurare uiciata reaedificare exaudi orationes nostras.', *PMC*, 128–9.

[31] *PMC*, 129.

- The bishop comes back into the church singing a psalm and antiphon, 'and the rest is as in the dedication of the church spelt out above.'[32] He blesses the altar and commends the holy place to the Lord, requesting that all wickedness in the future be eliminated from this place. The prayers which accompany this stage again use the language of restoration and cleansing.
- A solemn Mass follows immediately, in which the readings specified – the passage from the Book of Revelation (21:2–5a) about seeing a holy city, a new Jerusalem, coming down out of the heavens, and the parable from Luke (6:43–6) that no good tree bears bad fruit, nor a bad tree good fruit – allude to the importance of God's grace.[33] The prayers again continue the theme of cleansing from contamination and sanctifying place.[34]

The language used throughout is that of disease and pollution, including *spurcitia* (filthiness), *sordium* (filth), *culpa contagii* (contagion of sin), *maculatam* (taint) and *pollutio* (pollution).[35] This is a state which can only be rectified by cleansing and exorcism, hence the continuous requests that the Lord purge and purify the contamination.[36] The Canterbury rite also deliberately echoes and repeats elements from the rite for the original dedication of the church, hence the repeated cross-references to various elements in the dedication rite: the recitation of the litany, the exorcism, and the blessing of the altar.[37]

The rite is a very public and collective one. It begins outside the church with a procession, led by the bishop, but also involving the clergy and people: 'First the bishop comes before his church with the clergy and people singing this antiphon with a sonorous voice.'[38] The prayer texts repeatedly emphasise the collective nature of the service. The deacon instructs those present to genuflect after the bishop utters the initial prayer and then rise up; the prayers include a request that purity 'rise up in this place [since] this crowd of people agree to hold fast to their vows'. The rite ends by requesting the Lord to grant the request for restoration of purity to the crowd of people

---

[32] '*Deinde reportentur reliquiae ad aecclesiam psallendo. Ant.* Sanctum est uerum lumen. *Ut supra. Et reliqua sicut in dedicatione aecclesiae superius dictum est.*' *PMC*, 129.

[33] *PMC*, 131; e.g. for a summary of traditional interpretations of the passage in Revelation see Bede, *Commentary on Revelation*, ed. and trans. F. Wallis (Liverpool, 2013), 260–1 nn. 1028–33.

[34] *PMC*, 130–2.

[35] *PMC*, 127, 128, 129.

[36] See n. 30 above.

[37] *PMC*, 128, 129, 131.

[38] '*Primum ueniat episcopus ante ipsam aecclesiam cum clero et populo hanc sonora uoce canendo antiphonam*', *PMC*, 127.

making it.[39] It is also a rite which emphasises the bishop's authority. Only he can preside over the rite and reconcile this space, just as church dedication rites were reserved to the bishop.[40] Thus through this collective rite, in which bishop, clergy and people all call on the Lord to cleanse this space and make it sacred again, the church (and/or cemetery) is restored as a space suitable for the community of the living and the dead.

The rite in the Magdalen Pontifical represents the culmination of a series of liturgical changes across the later eighth, ninth, tenth and eleventh centuries.[41] The earliest evidence for a rite for the reconciliation of holy places is found in a group of three Gelasian sacramentaries compiled in France in the years around 800 CE.[42] This rite consists of two prayers under the rubric 'Reconciliation of the altar where killing has been carried out.' The orator requests that God restore, cleanse and purify the altar which has been polluted by this act.[43] The final request in the second prayer, that the 'pure simplicity of your church ... that has been defiled after receiving grace return to its glory', suggests that even at this early stage the altar already represented the whole

---

[39] '*Et diaconus. Flectamus genua. Leuate*'; 'Resurgat quesumus huius loci pura simplicitas et candore innocentiae restitutus dum pristinam recipit gratiam inuiolabilem reuertatur ad gloriam ut populorum huc turba conueniens dum petitionis hic ingerit uota uotorum se sentiat obtinuisse suffragia.' *PMC*, 128, 130. See also a reference to the requests of the crowd of people ('populorum turba') in one of the prayers to be said whilst processing three times around the inside and outside of the church or cemetery: *PMC*, 129.

[40] Gittos, *Liturgy*, 215.

[41] The history of the rites for reconciliation of defiled holy spaces has attracted much less attention than that for church dedications; for example, it is mentioned only in passing in Kozachek's helpful overview, 'Repertory of Chant'.

[42] Copied at Meaux *c.* 790–800 CE, Paris, BNdeF, Ms Lat. 12048: *Liber sacramentorum Gellonensis*, ed. Dumas and Deshusses, 351–2; copied near Trier *c.* 800, Berlin, Staatsbibliothek, MS Phillipps 1667: *Liber sacramentorum Augustodensis*, ed. Heiming, 165–6: 'CCCXL: Recontiliatio altaris ubi homicidium perpetrator.' The same sequence appears under the same heading in the Angoulême Pontifical as well: Paris, BNdeF, Ms lat. 816, *Liber sacramentorum Engolismensis*, ed. Saint-Roch, 304–5. For an overview of eighth-century Gelasian sacramentaries, which seem to have circulated widely in the late eighth- and ninth-century Frankish kingdoms, see Cyrille Vogel, *Medieval Liturgy: An Introduction to the Sources*, rev. and trans. W. G. Storey and N. K. Rasmussen (Washington, DC, 1986), 70–8; Bernard Moreton, *The Eighth-Century Gelasian Sacramentary: A Study in Tradition* (Oxford, 1976). A sacramentary is a book which includes only those prayer texts a priest (or bishop) needs to celebrate the Canon of the Mass and specific liturgical rites including church dedications; directions on *how* a particular rite should be conducted were reserved to a separate text, the *ordines*: Éric Palazzo, *A History of Liturgical Books from the Beginning to the Thirteenth Century*, trans. M. Beaumont (Collegeville, MN, 1998), 21–61; Vogel, *Medieval Liturgy*, 64–105.

[43] 'Ita auctoris nostri est lapsa restituere, mutantia stabilire ...', '... et altarem tuum quam insectantis est inimici fraude pollutum, per infusionem gratiae caelestis purificis, purificatumquem possedeas', *Liber sacramentorum Gellonensis*, ed. Dumas and Deshusses, 351–2 (nos. 2398–9).

church.[44] Rob Meens recently suggested that the appearance of this rite in late eighth-century Frankia should be linked to the emergence at the same time of a rite for the consecration of an altar;[45] and that both rites are a reflection, in the liturgy, of wider developments in Latin Christian thought and law over the course of the eighth century, which was when the idea that the church building should be regarded as sacred first became firmly established in ecclesiastical thought.[46]

Both Carolingian rulers and churchmen promoted two versions of the Roman liturgy: first the eighth-century Gelasian and then, under Charlemagne, in an effort to return to what they believed was a more authoritative rendering, the Gregorian sacramentary.[47] The Gregorian text was soon found wanting and a Frankish supplement to it compiled which includes blessings for the consecration of an altar. Various later ninth-century manuscripts of the Supplemented Gregorian include further prayers and *ordines* for the dedication of a church.[48] Whilst at least one example of the Supplemented Gregorian sacramentary includes a Mass for the reconciliation of a violated church, none of the manuscripts in this particular group includes any indication of a separate rite for the reconciliation of an altar or church which has been contaminated by an act of violence.[49]

Records of a full rite for the reconciliation of an altar or church contaminated by a violent act do not in fact reappear anywhere in the Latin West until the tenth century. When they do so, it is in England, and it is possible to trace the evolution of a specifically English rite across the next two centuries, from the mid-tenth to the mid-twelfth century. There are three main stages in the development of the written record of this rite across early English pontificals; these are collections of those rites reserved only to the bishop, such as clerical ordination as well as dedication of altars and churches.[50]

---

[44] 'Resurgat aecclesiae tuae pura simplicitas et candor innocentiae, hactenus maculatus dum recipit gratiam reuertatur ad gloriam', *ibid.*, 352 (no. 2399).

[45] Meens, 'Reconciling Disturbed Sacred Space'.

[46] Czock, *Gottes Haus*.

[47] On Gelasian and Gregorian sacramentaries see Vogel, *Medieval Liturgy*, 64–106; Palazzo, *History*, 35. For a revisionist account of their circulation and the limits of royal liturgical patronage see Yitzhak Hen, *The Royal Patronage of Liturgy in Frankish Gaul to the Death of Charles the Bald* (877), HBS Subsidia III (Woodbridge, 2001).

[48] *Le Sacramentaire grégorien. Ses principals formes d'après les plus anciens manuscrits*, 3rd edn, ed. J. Deshusses, Spicilegium Friburgense 16, 24, 28 (3 vols., Fribourg, 1988, 1992), I, 420–2, III, 176–94.

[49] 'Missa in reconciliatione ecclesiae', *Le Sacramentaire grégorien*, ed. Deshusses, III, 212, no. 461 (Paris, Bibliothèque nationale de France, n.a.l. 1589); this sacramentary is from late ninth-century Tours Cathedral and contains numerous additional texts.

[50] On early pontificals see N. K. Rasmussen, *Les Pontificaux du haut moyen âge. Genèse du livre de l'évêque*, ed. M. Haverals (Leuven, 1998).

The earliest two English examples of the rite are to be found in two manuscripts with connections to Worcester, now known as Claudius Pontifical I and the Egbert Pontifical.[51] Claudius I is a pontifical copied *c.* 1000 at Worcester, but seemingly based on an early tenth-century copy compiled at Canterbury.[52] The Egbert Pontifical was probably written for Oswald, bishop of Worcester (961–71).[53] The rite found in both these Worcester pontificals from the late tenth century is on the face of it a conservative text: the eighth-century Frankish Gelasian tradition of two prayers is accompanied by a 'Mass for the reconciliation of the church' drawn from the ninth-century Gregorian tradition.[54] The consequence was to extend the rite out from the altar to include other 'holy places', and in doing so move beyond the church building to incorporate also the reconciliation of cemeteries where blood had been spilt. We can follow this development in two places in the manuscript of the Egbert Pontifical. First the text of one of the original eighth-century Frankish Gelasian prayers, *Deus cuius bonitas*, has been amended to allow it to be used to reconcile a cemetery polluted in similar circumstances:

> God whose goodness has neither beginning nor end hear our prayers that that of yours which is polluted may be cleansed, that which is neglected restored, that which is damaged, rebuilt, so that you may accept as reconciled the shelter of this church or cemetery and your altar should be cleansed of the infestation of devilish deceit.[55]

Furthermore the noun chosen is not the usual *coemeterium*, but rather the archaic Frankish term *poliandrum*.[56] Secondly, the post-communion

---

[51] For the suggestion that these two pontificals 'evidently descend in parallel from a common ancestor' at Worcester see *The Sacramentary of Ratoldus (Paris, Bibliothèque nationale de France, lat. 12052)*, ed. N. Orchard, HBS 116 (2005), cii.

[52] London, BL, MS Cotton Claudius A. iii, ff. 77r–78v: *The Claudius Pontificals*, ed. D. H. Turner, HBS 97 (Chichester, 1971), 65–6.

[53] Paris, BNdeF, Ms Lat. 10575: *Two Anglo-Saxon Pontificals (the Egbert and Sidney Sussex Pontificals)*, ed. H. M. J. Banting, HBS 104 (1989), 60–1. Nicholas Orchard summarises the scholarship concluding the 'Egbert' Pontifical was 'associated with Oswald, bishop of Worcester (961–71)' in his edition of another tenth-century manuscript with strong textual links: *The Sacramentary of Ratoldus* ed. Orchard, cii.

[54] The text for the 'Missa in reconciliatione aecclesie' precedes the reconciliation rite prayers in Claudius I (*The Claudius pontificals*, 65) but succeeds them in the Egbert Pontifical (*Two Anglo-Saxon Pontificals*, 61).

[55] 'Deus cuius bonitas nec principium nec finem habet cuius est polluta purgare neglecta restaurare uitiata readificare exaudi orationes nostras ut huius aecclesiae siue poliandri receptaculum placatus accipas et altare tuum quod infestantis diaboli fraude fuit pollutum': *Two Anglo-Saxon Pontificals*, 60; for an image of this text in the manuscript see Paris, BNdeF, Ms Lat. 10575, f. 77r on *Gallica* (https://gallica.bnf.fr/ark:/12148/btv1b105422032/f159. item.r=latin%2010575, last accessed 23 June 2021); a second reference to the need to purify the *poliandrum* as well as the church was added to this prayer above the line by a second, more informal hand.

[56] On its use in Merovingian texts see J. F. Niermeyer, *Mediae latinitatis lexicon minus* (Leiden, 2001), 811. It is not ranked in the *Dictionary of Medieval Latin from British Sources*,

prayer in the Mass for the reconciliation of a church which follows was similarly amended later to request that the Lord ensure that this temple *or this cemetery* remains holy and protected from the defilements of barbarians and the unjust.[57] The 'Egbert Pontifical' has been linked on palaeographical grounds to Worcester *c.* 970, partly on the basis of the inclusion of texts also associated with Wulfstan, bishop of Worcester and archbishop of York (d. 1023), which include several archaic elements similar to the use of *poliandrum* here.[58]

The second stage in the development of this rite is found in the pontifical made for Archbishop Dunstan (959–88), probably at Canterbury in the 960s.[59] This example includes for the first time an instructional rubric to the bishop on how to conduct the rite 'for the reconciliation of holy places where blood has been spilt or killing perpetrated': 'the primate should sprinkle blessed water three times around and inside saying these prayers'.[60] The rite itself consists of the same two prayers first found in the late eighth-century Frankish Gelasian sacramentaries, followed by a new prayer in which the minister requests God to sanctify

meaning it appears fewer than fifty times in the corpus: dmlbs.ox.ac.uk (last accessed 7 March 2021). I am aware of only one other English usage: in a manuscript of the canon law collection often attributed to Archbishop Wulfstan: Cambridge, Corpus Christi College, Ms 265, p. 123, edited in Michael Elliot, 'Canon Law Collections in England, ca. 600–1066: The Manuscript Evidence' (Ph.D. thesis, University of Toronto, 2013), 877; the text of this canon is a direct copy of an early ninth-century Carolingian text, Theodulf of Orléans's *Capitula I*, c. 9 (*MGH Capitula Episcoporum*, I, ed. P. Brommer (Hanover, 1984), 109).

[57] 'ut templum hoc /uel poliandrum\ a barbarorum inquinamentis emundatum tua benedictione maneat', *Two Anglo-Saxon Pontificals*, 61; Paris, BNdeF, Ms Lat. 10575, f. 77v (*Gallica*, https://gallica.bnf.fr/ark:/12148/btv1b105422032/f160.item.r=latin%2010575, last accessed 23 June 2021).

[58] Palaeography: D. Dumville, 'Anglo-Saxon Books: Treasure in Norman Hands?', *Anglo-Norman Studies*, 16 (1994), 83–99, at 95 n. 59 (style of script is similar to a charter written at Worcester 969, S 1326; see n. 85 for details). Textual links to Wulfstan: C. A. Jones, 'Wulfstan's Liturgical Interests', in *Wulfstan, Archbishop of York: The Proceedings of the Second Alcuin Conference*, ed. M. Townend (Turnhout, 2004), 325–52, at 327–8, 343 (archaic); *idem*, 'The Chrism Mass in Later Anglo-Saxon England', in *The Liturgy of the Later Anglo-Saxon Church*, ed. Helen Gittos and M. Bradford Bedingfield, HBS Subsidia 5 (2005), 105–42 at 114–15, 120, 142; *idem*, 'The Origins of the "Sarum" Chrism Mass at Eleventh-Century Christ Church, Canterbury', *Mediaeval Studies*, 67 (2005), 219–315, at 234–5. Helen Gittos has suggested that the Egbert scribe selected materials from different sources and adapted them to accord with contemporary practice: *Liturgy*, 223.

[59] Paris, BNdeF, Ms lat. 943, ff. 62v–63v; a digitised copy of the manuscript is available through *Gallica* (gallica.bnf.fr, last accessed 7 March 2021); there is a transcription by M. A. Conn, 'The Dunstan and Brodie (Anderson) Pontificals: An Edition and Study' (Ph.D. thesis, University of Notre Dame, 1993), 107–12.

[60] 'Reconciliatio loci sacri ubi sanguis fuerit effusus aut homicidium perpetratum. *Primitus ter aspergat aquam benedictam in circuitu et intus et dicat has orationes …*', Paris, BNdeF, Ms 943, f. 62v.

this church or cemetery which he has already made holy previously.[61] The Latin here is the more usual *cymiterium*. Unlike the scribe of the Egbert Pontifical rite, that of the Dunstan Pontifical sought to include the cemetery as well as the church building in this reconciliation rite from the beginning. The Dunstan Pontifical is securely dated to Archbishop Dunstan's pontificate on grounds of script, contents (including a copy of the papal privilege granting him the pallium he collected from Rome on 21 September 960, in the same hand as the main text, and an *ordo* for consecrating an archbishop) and illustrations.[62]

The third stage in the development of this rite is to be found in two later pontificals, both associated with Canterbury and copied *c.* 1000: the so-called Benedictional of Archbishop Robert and the Anderson Pontifical.[63] The Anderson Pontifical, in particular, bears various marks that it was read closely. These comprise firstly a number of marginal additions including a marginal gloss to the rite for reconciliation of holy places where blood has been spilt which extends the rite explicitly to include cemeteries violated in the same way.[64] The same annotator also made reference to the singing of litanies, and specific antiphons. The antiphons cited are those more commonly used in contemporary English rites for the dedication of a church and consecration of a cemetery.[65] These marginal additions were written in a very similar hand to that of the main text, so why were such chant texts added, and by whom? The most probable answer is a pragmatic solution: they reflect actual occasions on which this rite was staged. Similar additions were made to the rites for the reconciliation of altars and holy places and the consecration of cemeteries in a pontifical written at Canterbury or

---

[61] 'ut hanc aecclesiam uel hoc cymiterium quod prius tua sanctificatione sanctificari uoluisti', Paris, BNdeF, Ms 943, f. 63v; Conn, 'The Dunstan and Brodie (Anderson) Pontificals', 108.

[62] Script: David Dumville, *Liturgy and the Ecclesiastical History of Late Anglo-Saxon England: Four Studies* (Woodbridge, 1992), 82; Jane Rosenthal, 'The Pontifical of St Dunstan', in *St Dunstan: His Life, Times and Cult*, ed. N. Ramsay, M. Sparks and T. Tatton-Brown (Woodbridge, 1992), 143–63, at 151.

[63] Rouen, Bibliothèque municipal, MS 369 (Y.7): *The Benedictional of Archbishop Robert*, ed. H. A. Wilson, HBS 24 (1903), 110–13; London, British Library, Additional Ms 57337; a digitised copy is available from the British Library (www.bl.uk/manuscripts/ FullDisplay.aspx?ref=Add_MS_57337, last accessed 21 February 2021), and a transcript in Conn, 'The Dunstan and Brodie (Anderson) Pontificals', 257–62.

[64] 'Benedictio cimiterium ubi sanguis effusus', London, BL, Additional Ms 57337, f. 53v.

[65] For example, the antiphon 'Asperges me' added in the margin to Anderson's rite (London, BL, Additional Ms 57337, f. 53v) is also found earlier in Anderson's rite for the consecration of a cemetery (*ibid.*, f. 34v) and in the rites for the dedication of a church, the consecration of a cemetery and of a cross in the Dunstan Pontifical (Paris, BNdeF, Ms lat. 943, ff. 16v, 42v, 75v) (*Cantus* ID 001494). Similar associations can be traced using the Cantus database for other antiphons mentioned in the marginal glosses to the Anderson reconciliation rite.

Winchester (now Cambridge, Corpus Christi College Ms 146) around the same time as Anderson.[66] Rites such as this were outside the normal temporal round of offices and Masses; the need to reconcile violated space was clearly not so routine that the community of Canterbury was able to undertake it without some planning. The cantor, the cleric tasked with staging a formal rite like this, is therefore the person most likely to have to consult the text ahead of time to consider how this rite should be enacted.[67] The later marginal notes of the antiphons to be sung – seemingly written in two stints – therefore probably signify that on at least two different occasions a cantor gave thought to how this rite should be delivered, and hint at the translation of written text into physical performance.

This evidence of revision, amplification and glossing suggests that these rites for the reconciliation of holy spaces where blood has been spilt were amended and updated across the second half of the tenth century and into the early eleventh century at Worcester and Canterbury. Each time, provision was made to expand the rite to incorporate the possibility that the sacred space which might be violated could include the cemetery as well as the church itself. The final major change in the evolution of the reconciliation rite in England came in the mid-eleventh century in a pontifical possibly made for the last pre-Norman archbishop, Stigand (1052–70).[68] This rite included new Continental elements from the Romano-German rite for the reconciliation of a violated church which seems to have developed independently, if contemporaneously, in tenth- and early eleventh-century east Frankia.[69] But the English rite departed from the Frankish Romano-German rite in one major way. The Frankish rite specified that, having blessed the water,

[66] Cambridge, Corpus Christi College, MS 146, pp. 93, 95; on its date see Gittos's summary in her *Liturgy*, 287–8.

[67] Margot Fassler, 'The Office of the Cantor in Early Western Monastic Rules and Customaries: A Preliminary Investigation', *Early Music History*, 5 (1985), 29–51; *Medieval Cantors and Their Craft: Music, Liturgy and the Shaping of History, 800–1500*, ed. K. A.-M. Bugyis, A. B. Kraebel and M. Fassler (Woodbridge, 2017).

[68] Cambridge, Corpus Christi College, Ms 44, pp. 174–86. For the dating and attribution to Stigand, see the summary in Gittos, *Liturgy*, 282, who makes clear that its rites for consecrating churches and cemeteries revise those present in two pontificals linked to Canterbury: London, British Library Ms Cotton Vitellius A.vii (>1030, Ramsey/Exeter) and British Library, Additional Ms 28188 (s. xi$^{3/4}$, Exeter copy).

[69] *Le Pontifical romano-germanique du dixième siècle*, ed. C. Vogel and R. Elze (3 vols., Vatican City, 1963, 1972), I, 182–5: 'Ordo L: *Reconciliatio violatae ecclesiae*'. Formerly dated to mid-tenth-century Mainz, the Romano-German pontifical is now attributed to early eleventh-century Bamberg: Henry Parkes, 'Henry II, Liturgical Patronage and the Birth of the Romano-German Pontifical', *Early Medieval Europe*, 28 (2000), 104–41; see 113 n. 34 for a summary of the development of this scholarly revision of the dating and origin of this compilation; Parkes describes the Romano-German pontifical as a 'collection of *spolia*', 128, but dates the church dedication rites in this compilation to the early eleventh century, 116–18.

salt, wine and ashes for exorcism, the bishop should go around the church three times on the inside, splashing the blessed water about, singing an antiphon and a psalm, in order to wash and purify the contaminated places.[70] The English version of this rite in Archbishop Stigand's mid-eleventh-century pontifical instead specifies that the bishop should go three times inside *and* three times outside the church or cemetery.[71] This requirement – that the bishop go outside – reflects a peculiarity of the English consecration rites, which also specify that the bishop lead three processions around the exterior of the church, rather than the more common single occasion in the Frankish tradition.[72] Indigenous English traditions clearly remained extremely powerful, even when Frankish elements were introduced into the reconciliation rites. This fourth version of the rite was in use for more than a century. It is almost identical to that in both the early twelfth-century pontifical made for Archbishop Anselm and the mid-twelfth-century Magdalen Pontifical.[73]

This review of reconciliation rites suggests first that the cathedral communities of churchmen in southern England – not just at Canterbury but also at Exeter and Worcester – in copying rites for the reconciliation of sacred places extended the remit of those rites to include violation of cemeteries from the second half of the tenth century onwards. Second, these communities reworked this material again and again across the later tenth, eleventh and twelfth centuries. They incorporated new elements from the Frankish tradition and from the chant tradition; they even offered alternative singular and plural readings of sacred places – oratory/oratories, church/churches, cemetery/cemeteries – in the prayers in Cambridge Corpus Christi College MS 44; this was presumably to help readers understand the importance of correct grammar in prayer rather than for practical use, as similar changes were made to the subsequent rite for blessing the baptistery to allow for the consecration of multiple baptisteries at once, a situation which seems highly unlikely, not to say unfeasible.[74] Whatever the reason for these revisions, they are all testimony to an ongoing interest in developing the rite.

[70] *Le Pontifical romano-germanique*, I, 183.

[71] 'In reconciliatione altaris uel sacri loci seu cimiterii … Postea circumeat tribus uicibis intrinsecus et extrinsecus aecclesiam vel cymiterium …' Cambridge, Corpus Christi College, Ms 44, pp. 174, 176–7.

[72] Gittos, *Liturgy*, 226.

[73] The only major difference is that the eleventh-century copyist of CCCC Ms 44, pp. 184–6, includes the *commendatio* at the end of the Mass following the rite, whilst his twelfth-century successors copied that *commendatio* at the end of the rite before the Mass; Dublin, Trinity College, Dublin, Ms 98, ff. 32v–33v; *PMC*, 130.

[74] Cambridge, Corpus Christi College, Ms 44, pp. 176, 178–9, 180, 181, 183–5, 186.

Their interest in the liturgy is echoed in church law. The medieval English church inherited a rich legacy of secular as well as earlier canon laws and penitentials.[75] The view that a place or building should be regarded as holy has deep roots in Roman tradition as well as early Christian doctrine and practice. In the Roman empire, the terms *dedicatio* and *consecratio* denoted a formal juridical procedure by which a site – a temple or a grave – was removed from secular use and became subject to divine law.[76] This idea that certain sites should be set apart as divine was carried over into early Christianity. The penitential associated with Theodore of Canterbury (d. 690) includes provision for sanctifying a church and cleansing it if a pagan is buried there.[77] At the same time, Roman law upheld the idea that such places should be inviolate; it condemned the violation of graves, for example, as a capital offence, and this teaching was taken over into medieval church law.[78] The contested nature of early Christianity also generated questions about the circumstances in which a church building might need to be reconsecrated. What happened if the building was destroyed by fire? What if the church had previously been in the hands of heretics? Was the original consecration valid? Should it be reconsecrated if the church was moved?[79]

Two specific problems inform a pair of canons which are first recorded in the mid-tenth century. If the altar had been moved should the church be reconsecrated? If the church had been violated by killing or an adulterous act should be it reconsecrated? The answer in both cases was yes. The earliest surviving record of this duo is from mid-tenth-century southern Germany; they first appear in England half a century later in the early eleventh-century records of a Worcester canon law collection, seemingly made for Archbishop Wulfstan.[80] Despite their apparent

---

[75] Patrick Wormald, *The Making of English Law: King Alfred to the Twelfth Century I: Legislation and Its Limits* (Oxford, 1999); Richard Helmholz, *The Oxford History of the Laws of England I: The History of the Canon Law and Ecclesiastical Jurisdiction, 597–1649* (Oxford, 2003), 1–143; Elliot, 'Canon Law Collections in England'.

[76] MacCormack, 'Loca Sancta', 257.

[77] 'Discipulus Umbrensium', II.1, 4–5, in *Die Canones Theodori Cantuariensis und ihre Überlieferungsformen*, ed. P. W. Finsterwalder (Weimar, 1929), 311–12.

[78] Dylan Elliott, 'Violence against the Dead: The Negative Translation and *Damnatio Memoriae* in the Middle Ages', *Speculum*, 92 (2017), 1020–55, at 1029–30.

[79] The historical summary in Gulczynski, *The Desecration*, 12–21, should be used with extreme caution as his identification and dating of canon law collections is now very outdated.

[80] '*Decreta Vigilii Papae*. Si motum fuerit altare denuo consecratur aecclesia. Si parietes motantur et non altare exorcizetur salibus tantum.' Munich, Bayerische Staatsbibliothek (BSB), Clm 6241, f. 33r (digitised at Münchener DigitalisierungsZentrum Digitale Bibliothek, www.digitale-sammlungen.de/en/view/bsb00078562?page=66,67, accessed 7 June 2021); this collection of extracts from the sixth-century *Epitome Hispana* collection

novelty, they represent developments from earlier traditions. Scholars of central medieval dedication rites have shown how they evolved out of earlier customs which separated dedication rites for the placing of relics in altars from those for the dedication of a church. A canon on the need for reconsecration when an altar has been moved is therefore not surprising; indeed the issue was raised in Theodore's Penitential and remained a live issue in canonical circles four centuries later as is testified by letters written by Ivo of Chartres (d. 1115) and Archbishop Anselm (d. 1109) about whether a church should be reconsecrated when an altar was moved, or only when it was removed.[81] Similarly, reconciliation rites for altars and holy spaces polluted by bloodshed and homicide survive, as we have seen, from the eighth century and are echoed in the provisions made in royal and ecclesiastical law in England and Frankia for punishing anyone killing someone in church from the ninth century onwards.[82] What seems more novel is the reference to the need to consecrate anew a holy place after an adulterous act had been committed there; whilst this canon entered church law, appearing in two of the most popular collections in eleventh- and twelfth-century Europe – Burchard's *Decretum* (*c.* 1020) and Gratian's *Decretum* (*c.* 1140) – the focus of the liturgical rites remained on pollution from bloodshed rather than sexual acts.[83] To return to these two canons:

was compiled in the last third of the tenth century in Freising: Lotte Kéry, *Canonical Collections of the Early Middle Ages (ca.400–1140): A Bibliographical Guide to the Manuscripts and Literature* (Washington, DC, 1999), 59; the pair also appear in other tenth/eleventh-century copies of this collection: Munich, BSB, Clm 3852, f. 65v (digitised at www.digi-tale-sammlungen.de/en/view/bsb00106135?page=130,131, accessed 7 June 2021) and Munich, BSB, Clm 3853, f. 134v (www.digitale-sammlungen.de/en/view/bsb00060190?page=272,273, accessed 7 June 2021). *Collectio Wigorniensis* A.3 (London, British Library, MS Cotton Nero A.i, f. 148r, digitised at British Library Digitised Manuscripts, www.bl.uk/manuscripts/Viewer.aspx?ref=cotton_ms_nero_a_i_f070r, accessed 7 June 2021): '*Virgilius Papa*. Si motum fuerit altare denuo consecretur ecclesia. Si parietes tantum mutantur, et non altare sane [*sic*] et aqua exorcizetur. Si homicidio vel adulterio fuerit uiolata diligentissime expurgetur et denuo consecretur.' For edition see Elliot, 'Canon Law Collections in England', 1025. The false attribution to Vigilius is perhaps related to Vigilius's letter to the Bishop of Braga on the circumstances in which a church should be reconsecrated, found in the ninth-century collection of Pseudo-Isidore: *Decretales Pseudo-Isidorianae et Capitula Angilramni*, ed. P. Hinschius (Leipzig, 1863), 711.

[81] Ep. LXXII, *PL* 162, 101–2; Ep. CLIX, *PL* 159, 194–5; Gulczynski, *Desecration*, 16–17.

[82] Frankia: Ansegis, *Collectio Capitularium*, IV.13, *Die Kapitulariensammlung*, ed. G. Schmitz, MGH Capitularia nova series 1 (Hanover, 1996), 625–7 (completed before 827); Regino of Prüm, *Libri Duo de Synodalibus Causis et Disciplinis Ecclesiasticis*, ed. F. G. A. Wasserschleben, rev. W. Hartmann (Darmstadt, 2004), II.31, 264 (completed *c.* 906). England: Laws of Alfred (*c.* 885 × 899), c. 5, and VIII Æthelred (1014), c. 1.1, *Councils and Synods with Other Documents Relating to the English Church I: AD 871–1204*, ed. D. Whitelock, M. Brett and C. N. L. Brooke (2 vols., Oxford, 1981), I, 24–5, 387–8.

[83] Burchard of Worms, *Decretum*, III.11–12, *PL* 140, 675; Gratian, Decretum, Pars III, D.I, c. xix (https://geschichte.digitale-sammlungen.de//decretum-gratiani, last accessed 10 March 2021). On the latter see the exploration of this trope and its later medieval history

they suggest that it is only from the second half of the tenth century that churchmen, first in Germany, then in England, became interested in prescribing that churches which had been violated by sinful acts should be cleansed and consecrated anew. When combined, the evidence of the liturgical rites and canon law indicates that English bishops and their clergy at Canterbury and Worcester became particularly interested in the rite for the reconciliation of holy spaces which have been violated in the later tenth century, and in extending this rite to include cemeteries around the year 1000. In the last part of this paper I therefore wish to consider why English churchmen began to pay attention to this rite at this time and in this way.

Bishop murder was extremely rare, but churches, the courtyards (*atria*) in front of them and cemeteries next to them were often sites for violent and destructive activities in the tenth and eleventh centuries. For example, the *Anglo-Saxon Chronicle* records how in 1002 King Æthelred II ordered that 'all Danish men who were in England [were] to be slain'; this is an event known to modern historians as the St Brice's Day Massacre.[84] What this meant in specific terms is made clear in the records of St Frideswide's church in Oxford. They include a charter issued by Æthelred in 1004 in favour of St Frideswide's which records how as a consequence of his royal decree a group of Danes sought sanctuary in the church whereupon the townspeople burnt it down.[85] All the community's records were consequently destroyed, hence the need for a new charter. The discovery in 2008 in nearby St John's College of a mass grave of some thirty-four men who had died by violence sometime between 960 and 1020 has been linked by archaeologists to this massacre.[86] Their skeletons are tangible evidence of the reality of such an event. Unfortunately liturgical texts are not as amenable as bones to radiocarbon dating when it comes to dating them precisely.

Even if we cannot link rites to particular events, stories widely reported in miracle accounts, chronicles and letter collections from across England, northern France, the Low Countries and east Frankia point

in Dyan Elliot, 'Sex in Holy Places: An Exploration of Medieval Anxiety', *Journal of Women's History*, 6 (1994), 6–34.

[84] Anglo-Saxon Chronicle (C, D, E versions), a. 1002: *The Anglo-Saxon Chronicle Ms C*, ed. K. O'Brien O'Keeffe, The Anglo-Saxon Chronicle: A Collaborative Edition 5 (Cambridge, 2001), 89; for a recent account see Levi Roach, *Æthelred the Unready* (New Haven and London, 2016), 187–200.

[85] S 909, *The Electronic Sawyer: Online Catalogue of Anglo-Saxon Charters* (https://esawyer.lib. cam.ac.uk, last accessed 18 February 2021); trans. *English History Documents 1: c. 500–1042*, 2nd edn, ed. and trans. D. Whitelock (1979), no. 127, 590–3.

[86] Sean Wallis, *The Oxford Henge and Late Saxon Massacre: with Medieval and Later Occupation at St John's College, Oxford* (Reading, 2014); Roach, *Æthelred*, 198–9.

to how churches and their precincts were often the site of violent acts in this period. In 1060, monks from the Flemish monastery of Lobbes took the relics of their patron, St Ursmer, on a tour of Flanders in order to re-establish their authority over their scattered properties after the disruption caused by conflict between the emperor and the count of Flanders, and to raise funds for rebuilding their church.[87] In St-Omer they encountered two rival parties of armed men surrounding the church of Blaringhem:

> The shields glinted red as the rays of the morning sun struck the courtyard (*atrium*) of the church as the steel of the weapons glistened, horses were snorting and whinnying, adding to the confusion.[88]

On enquiry the monks discovered the cause of this tension: two knights had quarrelled and initially been reconciled in the presence of the local count, but one knight, still unhappy, killed the other and then sought sanctuary in Blaringhem church. The count and his men then returned intending to take the killer captive for challenging his authority, whilst the other group sought to defend him. The monks passed through the armed men, entered the church, where they celebrated Mass, and then processed outside, placing St Ursmer's relics in the midst of the crowd and provoking a mass declaration of peace in which, so the author of the *Miracles of St Ursmer* recorded, more than one hundred feuds were ended. Not all cases ended so peacefully. Around 1020 the sub-dean of Chartres was murdered in the *atrium* in front of the cathedral as he was coming to church one night; this became a cause célèbre as Bishop Fulbert of Chartres accused the Bishop of Senlis of having organised the assassination together with his mother and brother, because they thought the post should have gone to the brother.[89] This story reveals a good deal about the tensions over family control of cathedral

---

[87] *Miracula S. Ursmari in itinere per Flandriam facta*, ed. O. Holder-Egger, MGH SS 15.2 (Hanover, 1888), 837–42; this is an abbreviated version of the text edited by G. Henschen in *Acta Sanctorum quotquot toto orbe coluntur*, ed. J. Bolland et al. (Antwerp, 1643–1971), 2 April, 573–8, trans. G. Koziol, in *Medieval Hagiography: An Anthology*, ed. T. Head (New York and London, 2001), 341–58. On this text see G. Koziol, 'Monks, Feuds, and the Making of Peace in Eleventh-Century Flanders', in *The Peace of God: Social Violence and Religious Response in France around the Year 1000*, ed. T. Head and R. Landes (Ithaca, 1992), 239–58.

[88] English translation by Koziol, in *Medieval Hagiography*, ed. Head, 348: 'Rubebat scutis totum atrium repercussione matutini solis splendebat acies armorum, confusior erat fremitus et hinnitus equorum.': *Miracula S. Ursmari*, ed. Holder-Egger, c. 6, 839.

[89] 'in ipso atrio principalis ecclesiae trucidarunt': *The Letters and Poems of Fulbert of Chartres*, ed. and trans. F. Behrends (Oxford, 1976), no. 29, 54; E. Peters, 'The Death of the Subdean: Ecclesiastical Order and Disorder in Eleventh-Century Francia', in *Law, Custom and the Social Fabric in Medieval Europe: Essays in Honour of Bryce Lyon*, ed. B. S. Bachrach and D. M. Nicholas (Kalamazoo, 1990), 51–71.

offices, but both tales also suggest that the courtyards in front of churches were not only public spaces, but potentially dangerous ones.[90]

Nor were the insides of churches safe places for members of the clergy and their households. In a case which shocked the north Italian clergy and the Ottonian court, Arduin, Margrave of Ivrea, killed Peter, Bishop of Vercelli, in his cathedral on 18 March 997, and burnt Peter's remains, incurring a sentence of excommunication.[91] But, as we have already seen at Chartres, churchmen might also be responsible for perpetrating violence within the church itself. Some sixty-five years later, violence erupted as a consequence of a seating-plan dispute between two important Ottonian churchmen: Abbot Widerad of the wealthy Rhineland monastery of Fulda and Bishop Hezelo of the Saxon see of Hildesheim. The incident took place at the Whitsun royal court at Goslar. The bishop of Hildesheim was unhappy about an incident which had occurred the previous Christmas, in which his claim to sit closest to the leading churchman in the east Frankish Church, the archbishop of Mainz, at vespers had been dismissed in favour of the abbot of Fulda. In order to prevent the same seating plan being enacted again, the bishop therefore arranged for one of his counts, a certain Ekbert, to hide behind an altar with several knights. When it became clear that the bishop's claims were again being challenged by the abbot of Fulda, Ekbert and his men leapt out and began fighting the abbot's men with cudgels and drove them out of the church. The men of Fulda then gathered their weapons and returned, bursting into the church during vespers as the brethren were singing psalms in the choir, and started fighting, this time with swords, causing 'rivers of blood' to run through the church. Two men, one on each side, were killed in the ensuing melee: the standard-bearer of the abbot and one of the bishop's knights. The bishop's men were again victorious, and again the Fulda men regrouped occupying the churchyard drawn up in a battle line; only night led to an end to the stand-off. The next day an investigation was held under royal auspices. The abbot was blamed, being accused of having come prepared for a fight with a large force; he and his men were forced to pay punitive fines to the king to retain their offices, and these were so steep that they impoverished the abbey for years to come. This account comes from the monk Lampert

---

[90] Fear of the consequent violence may be a hitherto unnoticed feature of the 1023 east Frankish Council of Seligenstadt's prohibition against people holding *colloquia* in church *atria*, instead of prayers and divine office; a *colloquium* generally refers to a court or synod: *Die Konzilien Deutschlands und Reichsitaliens*, ed. D. Jasper, MGH Concilia VIII (Hanover, 2010), 39.

[91] Ursula Brunhofer, *Arduin von Ivrea und seine Anhänger: Untersuchungen zum letzten italienischen Königtum des Mittelalters* (Augsburg, 1999), 80–5; For a recent account of this case see Levi Roach, *Forgery and Memory at the End of the First Millennium* (Princeton, 2021), 193–255.

of Hersfeld; he used the language of the Romano-German liturgical reconciliation rite, describing how the bishop 'with so much bloodshed ... avenged the injuries of the violated church (*violatae aecclesiae*)', hinting at the ecclesiastical discourse which presumably followed these events.[92]

These five cases are indicative of how in the tenth and eleventh centuries churches across the Latin West were the location for different sorts of violent clashes between armed men, attacks on unarmed men and attacks by angry mobs. Nor were such clashes confined to laymen; as both the Chartres and Goslar incidents suggest, churchmen themselves, even if they did not take part in the violence directly, could be accused of being its instigators. Stories such as these therefore provide one context for this ecclesiastical interest in recording and developing, if not creating, a liturgy for the reconciliation of such violated places. To put it simply, through administering such a rite, bishops were able to reassert their authority as arbiters of sacredness where it had been challenged by the violation of sacred space. The bishop's position as spiritual leader of the diocese was articulated from the moment he processed with the crowd in front of the church at the beginning of the rite, and reinforced as he physically cleansed and purified the boundaries of the holy spaces with holy water. Doing so helped him to reassert his own authority in setting the church and cemetery apart from lay society at a time of friction. Scholars have noted that other rites – the chrism Mass, public penance, church dedication rites, excommunication – which similarly articulated and promoted episcopal authority over the diocesan clergy and laity evolved around the same time (the later tenth and eleventh centuries) as that for the reconciliation of places polluted by violence, most noticeably in England, but also in north-east France, the Reich and Italy.[93]

---

[92] 'Tum vero urgebat et ille apostolicae sanctitatis ac Mosaicae mansuetudinis episcopus, qui tanti sanguinis effusione manus suas Deo consecraverat et violatae aecclesiae iniurias truculentius atque inmitius quam rex suas persequabatur': Lampert of Hersfeld, *Annales*, a. 1063, *Lamperti monachi Hersfeldensis Opera*, ed. O. Holder-Egger, MGH SRG 38 (Hanover and Leipzig, 1894), 83. Compare: *Le Pontifical romano-germanique*, I, 182–5. Sixty years later William of Malmesbury, writing in southern England, presumed that the cathedral was cleansed (*purgatam*), although he only described the Mass for Pentecost which followed in detail: 'Sed statim episcopis conuolantibus pace inter reliquias dissidentium statuta templum purgatum, missa festiuis clamoribus acta': William of Malmesbury, *Gesta regum anglorum*, II.192, ed. R. A. B. Mynors, R. M. Thomson and M. Winterbottom (2 vols., Oxford, 1998), I, 344.

[93] C. A. Jones, 'The Chrism Mass in Later Anglo-Saxon England', in *The Liturgy of the Late Anglo-Saxon Church*, ed. H. Gittos and M. Bradford Bedingfield, HBS Subsidia 5 (2005), 105–42, especially his observation that 'A heightening of liturgical and canonical emphasis on the consecration of oils can be seen as a kind of episcopal insurance policy, or guarantee of sustained control over proliferating smaller churches', *ibid.*, 131; S. Hamilton, 'Rites for Public Penance in Late Anglo-Saxon England', in *The Liturgy*, ed. Gittos and Bedingfield, 65–103, at 87–8; S. Hamilton, 'The Early Pontifical: The Anglo-Saxon Evidence Reconsidered from a Continental Perspective', in *England and the Continent in the Tenth Century: Studies in*

This interest in promoting episcopal authority over what constituted sacred space and how it should be restored following violent bloodshed in late tenth-century England fits with the model which Tom Lambert has recently proposed for the overall judicial landscape of post-Alfredian England:

> We should, I believe, think of Anglo-Saxon England as a society in which violence ... was regulated not by prohibitions imposed by a single central authority, but by a network of protections emanating from numerous different sources ...[94]

The tenth and eleventh centuries, in Lambert's view, witnessed an expansion of claims to royal protection, and at the same time, kings reserved the most heinous offences, including homicide within a church building, to their own jurisdiction. But this world of overlapping lordly protections, in which different authorities claimed jurisdiction over different spaces, and in which kings often asserted their jurisdiction in ecclesiastical spheres for the church's protection, provides a suitable context for, and explains, the seemingly precocious English interest in documenting – in law and liturgy – bishops' control over reconsecrating spaces violated by violence.

To date, modern researchers' focus has largely been on the ways in which west Frankish tenth- and eleventh-century churchmen responded to violent attacks. They have traced how monks responded to attacks on, and invasions of, church property both through the recitation of long, elaborate liturgical curses – the monastic *clamor* – and through an elaborate ritual in which they humiliated saints' relics;[95] how bishops had recourse to excommunication of enemies in defence of their property;[96]

*Honour of Wilhelm Levison (1876–1947)*, ed. D. Rollason, C. Leyser and H. Williams (Turnhout, 2010), 411–28; Gittos, *Liturgy*, 212–56; S. Hamilton, 'Medieval Curses and Their Users', *Haskins Society Journal*, 30 (2018), 21–51. On these developments in continental Europe at the same time see N. K. Rasmussen, 'Célébration épiscopale et célébration presbyterale: une essai de typologie', *Segni e riti nella chiesa altomedievale occidentale: 11–17 aprile 1985*, Settimane 33 (Spoleto, 1987), 581–603; *idem*, *Les Pontificaux*; Éric Palazzo, *L'Évêque et son image. L'illustration du pontifical au Moyen Âge* (Turnhout, 1999), 17–35; *idem*, 'La liturgie de l'Occident médiéval autour de l'an mil: État de la question', *Cahiers de civilisation médiéval*, 43 (2000), 371–94; Louis I. Hamilton, *A Sacred City: Consecrating Churches and Reforming Society in Eleventh-Century Italy* (Manchester, 2010).

[94] T. B. Lambert, 'Royal Protections and Private Justice: A Reassessment of Cnut's "Reserved Pleas"', in *English Law before Magna Carta: Felix Liebermann and Die Gesetze der Angelsachsen*, ed. S. Juranski, L. Oliver and A. Rabin (Leiden, 2010), 157–75, at 169.

[95] Lester K. Little, *Benedictine Maledictions: Liturgical Cursing in Romanesque France* (Ithaca, 1993); Patrick Geary, 'Humiliation of Saints', in his *Living with the Dead in the Middle Ages* (Ithaca, 1994), 95–115 (originally published in French in *Annales: ESC*, 34 (1979), 27–42); *idem*, 'Living with Conflicts in Stateless France: A Typology of Conflict Management Mechanisms, 1050–1200', in his *Living with the Dead*, 125–60 (originally published in French in *Annales: ESC*, 41 (1986), 1107–33).

[96] Hamilton, 'Medieval Curses and Their Users'; *eadem*, '*Absoluimus uos uice beati petri apostolorum principis*: Episcopal Authority and the Reconciliation of Excommunicants in England

and how bishops and monks came together in the Peace of God councils from the end of the tenth century to articulate and defend the defenceless – clergy and the poor, women and children – from violent attack on persons and property.[97] The rite for the reconciliation of sacred places where blood has been spilt therefore needs to be added to this list. The extent to which other ecclesiastical defensive actions are a result of, and reaction to, political transition and the weakness of royal authority – particularly because so many of them are concentrated in west Frankia – has been the subject of considerable debate.[98] The marked monastic bias of much of this evidence has been less discussed. Research on other forms of ecclesiastical defence against theft and violence relies on charter, legal and narrative evidence, or exceptional liturgical texts for the *clamor* and *humiliatio*, rather than texts routinely copied in liturgical collections. The rites for the reconciliation of sacred places where blood has been spilt help, therefore, to provide a useful corrective to this picture: for these rites are usually copied next to rites for the dedication of churches in sacramentaries and pontificals written across the Latin West.[99] They are thus normative and routine elements of these collections, but this should not mean they should be ignored. Rather their existence is a consequence of particular points in time in the legal and social history of the Latin medieval West. Additionally, the precocious evolution of this rite in late tenth-century southern English cathedrals offers a new perspective on a picture too long dominated by the experience of French monasticism.

Liturgy's formulaic and apparently timeless nature has for too long been regarded as an obstacle to its use as meaningful historical evidence, when in fact it is a strength as it allows, as we have seen, for the systematic comparison of changes in ecclesiastical thought and practice over both time and space.[100] Moreover we should not ignore a genre which constitutes the most plentiful category of texts to survive from England in the

and Francia, c. 900–1150', in *Frankland: The Franks and the World of the Early Middle Ages. Essays in Honour of Dame Jinty Nelson* (Manchester, 2008), 209–41; *eadem*, 'Law and Liturgy: Excommunication Records, 900–1050', in *Using and Not Using the Past after Carolingian Empire, c. 900–c. 1050*, ed. S. Greer, A. Hicklin and S. Esders (Abingdon, 2020), 282–302.

[97] *The Peace of God*, ed. Head and Landes (Ithaca, 1992); Geoffrey Koziol, *The Peace of God* (Leeds, 2018).

[98] For summaries of this debate see Charles West, *Reframing the Feudal Revolution: Political and Social Transformation between Marne and Moselle, c. 800–c. 1100* (Cambridge, 2013), 1–4, and D. Barthélemy, 'Revisiting the "Feudal Revolution" of the Year 1000', in his *The Serf, the Knight and the Historian*, trans. G. R. Edwards (Ithaca, 2009), 1–11.

[99] As is clear from the examples of early Frankish and English pontificals described by Rasmussen, *Les Pontificaux*, 53, 147, 198–9, 267–8.

[100] M. Fassler, 'The Liturgical Framework of Time and the Representation of History', in *Representing History, 900–1300: Art, Music, History*, ed. R. A. Maxwell (University Park, 2010), 149–71.

tenth and eleventh centuries.[101] That entire codices, such as those considered above, represent only the visible surface of a large iceberg is indicated by the plentiful fragments preserved in later medieval and early modern book bindings and record wrappings which are still coming to light. But in a world in which parchment was expensive, and writing highly skilled, the decision to record any rite was always a self-conscious one. Asking why, in what was still a predominantly oral world, any rite was written down is an obvious, but curiously neglected, question. In a society which valued memory, these written records were not simple scripts for conducting worship, but instead served different and overlapping purposes: as instruments for meditative reflection on a theme, for instruction, and for the articulation of claims to authority.[102] Tracing how particular rites such as this one were recorded and revised by anonymous copyists allows modern scholars to trace the evolution of ideas and the development of intellectual culture for the many known and unknown churchmen whose daily lives were shaped by the liturgy.

But let us return to where we began, with the reconciliation of Canterbury Cathedral eleven months after Becket's murder. That rite was not a Roman import but rather the latest iteration of a much longer tradition of a rite in which bishops reasserted their authority when church buildings were desecrated. The churchmen of the southern English province would already have been familiar with some form of this rite. The reason why this service was so delayed was because papal guidance was sought about what should be done in the absence of an archbishop to administer the rite. The legates and Canterbury community asked advice not because they did not know what to do when a church was desecrated by a killing, but rather because they were unclear as to who should lead the rite in this particular case; this rite was so indelibly linked in their minds to the articulation of episcopal authority that they were unclear who should conduct it in Becket's place.

---

[101] For example, some 36 per cent of the entries in the most recent handlist of early English manuscripts, 464 out of a total of 1,291, pertain to liturgical books: Helmut Gneuss and Michael Lapidge, *Anglo-Saxon Manuscripts: A Bibliographical Handlist of Manuscripts and Manuscript Fragments Written or Owned in England up to 1100* (Toronto, 2014); I used Gneuss and Lapidge's definition of liturgical books in their index.

[102] Henry Parkes, *The Making of Liturgy in the Ottonian Church: Books, Music and Ritual in Mainz, 950–1050* (Cambridge, 2015), 2–7, 218–23; Helen Gittos, 'Researching the History of Rites', in *Understanding Medieval Liturgy: Essays in Interpretation*, ed. Helen Gittos and Sarah Hamilton (Farnham, 2016), 13–37, at 20–23; Sarah Hamilton, 'Interpreting Diversity: Excommunication Rites in the Tenth and Eleventh Centuries', *ibid.*, 125–58.

*Transactions of the RHS* 31 (2021), pp. 49–73 © The Author(s), 2021. Published by Cambridge University Press on behalf of the Royal Historical Society. This is an Open Access article, distributed under the terms of the Creative Commons Attribution-NonCommercial-NoDerivatives licence (https://creativecommons.org/licenses/by-nc-nd/4.0/), which permits non-commercial re-use, distribution, and reproduction in any medium, provided the original work is unaltered and is properly cited. The written permission of Cambridge University Press must be obtained for commercial re-use or in order to create a derivative work.
doi:10.1017/S0080440121000037

# BAROQUE AROUND THE CLOCK: DANIELLO BARTOLI SJ (1608–1685) AND THE USES OF GLOBAL HISTORY*

## By Simon Ditchfield

READ 18 SEPTEMBER 2020

ABSTRACT. Right from its foundation in 1540, the Society of Jesus recognised the value and role of visual description (ekphrasis) in the persuasive rhetoric of Jesuit missionary accounts. Over a century later, when Jesuit missions were to be found on all the inhabited continents of the world then known to Europeans, descriptions of the new-found lands were being read for the entertainment as well as the edification of their Old World audiences. The first official history of the Society's missions in the vernacular, the volumes authored by Daniello Bartoli (1608–1685), played an important role in communicating a sense of the distinctiveness of the order's global mission. Referred to by Giacomo Leopardi (1798–1837) as the 'Dante of baroque prose', Bartoli developed a particularly variegated and intensely visual idiom to meet the challenge of describing parts of the world which the majority of his readers, including himself, would never visit.

There has never been a better time to write about the history of the Jesuits. As the footnotes to this paper demonstrate, the last twenty years or so, in particular, has seen a renaissance in the study not only of the old (pre-suppression) Society but also of the order after its refounding in 1814. This has culminated in the recent publication of two major reference works, by Cambridge and Oxford University Presses, in 2017 and 2019 respectively.[1] Although not a few of the scholars who have

---

*For John O'Malley, in gratitude and affection, on his ninety-fourth birthday.

[1] *The Cambridge Encyclopedia of the Jesuits*, ed. Thomas Worcester (Cambridge, 2017); *The Oxford Handbook of the Jesuits*, ed. Ines G. Županov (Oxford, 2019). The 'opening out' of Jesuit studies to non-Jesuits is widely accepted to have begun with the first of two big conferences on the Society hosted by Boston College in 1997, which issued in the volume of proceedings, *Jesuits: Cultures, Arts and the Sciences, 1540–1773*, ed. J. W. O'Malley *et al.* (Toronto, Buffalo and London, 1999). See the reflections on the proceedings made by Luce Giard (*ibid.*, 709–10), who used the more resonant French term '*désenclavement*'.

played (and continue to play) an active and distinguished part in this revival are themselves members of the Society, including the dedicatee of this paper, the field of Jesuit studies is now a genuinely ecumenical enterprise, open to scholars both religious and lay, from all disciplines, who work in all four corners of the globe, as befits a religious order that, as this paper goes on to discuss, has contributed in such fundamental ways to meeting the challenge for people of European heritage of discovering how to describe a vastly expanded world in the early modern period. The Jesuits were careful to write their own history from the very beginning of their existence, starting with the so-called 'autobiography' of their founder (which was actually written up from memory by Luis Gonçalves da Camara at the end of each day during which he had been listening to Ignatius give an account of his life[2]).

So when the focus of this essay, Daniello Bartoli, put pen to paper he was already heir to a rich tradition. However, it was a largely latinate tradition, and he was the first to offer a vernacular account which, on the one hand, enjoyed official status and, on the other, covered those parts of the globe where the Jesuit missionaries had either distinguished themselves mainly through heroic defeat and martyrdom – namely Asia (India, Southeast Asia and Japan) and England – or as in China showed themselves to be, at least on the Jesuits' own account, superior to even the Confucian-educated elite. Bartoli created a rich resource to inspire his confreres when read out loud at refectories in the Italian peninsula and beyond, or as a prose model to be borrowed by preachers, imitated by hagiographers or simply to be admired and copied (and maybe even translated into Latin) by students attending the dense network of Jesuit colleges for at least two centuries after Bartoli's death.[3]

# I

Sir, here is what I promised you. Here is the first outline of the morality of the good Jesuit fathers, 'these men, outstanding in doctrine and in wisdom, who are guided by divine wisdom which is more certain than all philosophy, which is more infallible than all the rules of philosophy.' You may think that I am joking, but I say this quite seriously, or rather they say it themselves. I am simply copying down their own words, in their

---

[2]  For this reason, the editor of the latest edition in English translation stops calling this work an 'autobiography' and instead gives it the following title: *A Pilgrim's Testament: The Memoirs of St Ignatius of Loyola*, ed. Barton T. Geger (Boston, MA, 2020). My thanks to Dr Thomas Flowers SJ for alerting me to this important detail.

[3]  That Bartoli's work was still deemed relevant and commercially viable after the restoration of the Society in 1814, at least in the Italian peninsula, can be seen by the edition of his complete works in thirty-four octavo volumes printed in Turin by Giacinto Marietti (1825–43), whose first eighteen volumes consisted of the *Istoria*, published all together in 1825. There is no extant evidence to suggest that Bartoli ever began work on the volumes of the *Istoria* which would have covered the Americas.

work entitled, *Imago primi saeculi*. I am only transcribing from them and from the close of their Elogium. 'This is the society of men, or rather of angels, predicted by Isaiah in these words: "Go, ye angels, prompt and swift of wing."' Is not the prophecy, as applicable to them, clear? 'They are eagle-spirits; they are a flight of phoenixes (for a recent author has shown that there is more than one phoenix). They have changed the face of Christendom.' Since they assert all this, we are bound to believe them.[4]

In this way, the French philosopher Blaise Pascal (1623–1662) put his finger on a problem that has not gone away in the intervening centuries: are we bound to believe the Jesuits' account of their own history and achievements?[5] The immediate occasion for Pascal's coruscating wit was his defence of the Jansenist Antoine Arnauld (1612–1694), and the quotation is taken from the opening lines of the fifth provincial letter, dated 20 March 1656. Pascal was himself quoting from that great monument to Jesuit pride, as well as to the arts of engraving and Latin encomia, which was the 952-folio-page *Image of the First Century* (*Imago Primi Saeculi*) published by the Flandro-Belgian province to accompany celebration of their first centenary in 1640 and embellished with no fewer than 127 emblems.[6] The emblem that perhaps more than any other emphasises the global scope of Jesuit missionary ambition is 'One world is not enough' (*Unus non sufficit orbis*) (Figure 1).[7] It has its counterpart in the frontispiece to the second edition of the opening volume of the first vernacular history of the Society's founder, the Basque nobleman and knight Ignatius of Loyola (*c*.1491–1556), by the subject of this article, the Ferrarese Jesuit Daniello Bartoli (1608–1685).[8] Bartoli's approach to his subject was faithfully represented in the work's distinctive title, *Della Vita e del Istituto di S. Ignazio fondatore della Compagnia di Giesu* ('The Life and Order/Rule of Life of St Ignatius, founder of the Company of Jesus'), and its frontispiece in which

---

[4] Blaise Pascal, *The Provincial Letters*, trans. A. J. Krailsheimer (Harmondworth, 1967), 74. I have slightly adapted Krailsheimer's translation. My reference text has been the Flammarion edition with notes by Antoine Adam: *Lettres écrites à un provincial* (Paris, 1967), 73.

[5] 'Il le faut croire puis qu'ils le disent', *Lettres*, 73.

[6] *Imago Primi Saeculi Societatis Iesu a Provincia Flandro-Belgica eiusdem Societatis Repraesenta* (Antwerp, 1640).

[7] *Ibid.*, 326.

[8] The first published history of the Society was the two Latin volumes by Niccolò Orlandini (who died in 1606), which were completed by Franceso Sacchini and published in 1614 and 1621. The first of these was, in turn, heavily dependent on Juan Alfonso de Polanco's account of the life of Ignatius and the activities of the Society in the period 1537–56, the *Chronicon Societatis Iesu*, which remained unpublished until the six-volume edition in the Monumenta Historica Societatis Iesu series (Madrid, 1894–8). Sacchini took the story down to Ignatius's successor, Superior General Diego Laínez (in office 1558–65). Sacchini also contributed to volume 3, which was published only in 1649. This covered the period 1564–72. Volume 4 followed three years later, in 1652, and covered the period 1572–80. The first part of volume 5 (1580–90) was revised by Pierre Poussines and published in 1661.

Figure 1. *Unus non sufficit orbis* (One world is not enough). Taken from *Imago primi saeculi Societatis Iesu a Prouincia Flandro-Belgica euisdem Societatis repreasentata* (Antwerp: Ex officina Plantiniana Balthasaris Moreti, 1640), 326. Image courtesy of the Pius XII Memorial Library, St Louis.

Ignatius has become the very symbol and embodiment of a religious order which directs the divine illumination from the fixed stars (Figure 2). Not for nothing had Bartoli been taught by the most brilliant anti-Copernican of the seventeenth century, his fellow Jesuit and Ferarrese Giovanni Battista Riccioli (1598–1671), so that Ignatius shone – or as Bartoli puts it in the note to the reader 'sounded' (*Ignatium sonant*) – throughout the world by reaching all four parts of the globe represented here by personifications of Africa, Asia, Europe and the Americas.

## II

On the very first page of the address to the reader of the first edition of this work, Bartoli noted how the foundation and progress of the Society could be mapped onto the entire known world: Spain being the place of Ignatius's birth; France of his education, together with that of his first companions, at the Sorbonne in Paris; Italy as the location of the Society's foundation by Pope Paul III; Portugal as the site of preparations for its first overseas missions. Germany, meanwhile, witnessed the

Figure 2. *Historia della compagnia di Gesù del R.P. Daniello Bartoli della medesima compagnia. Anteportam* by Jan Miel and Cornelis Bloemaert (Rome: de Lazzari, 1659). Image courtesy of the Archivum Historicum Societatis Iesu (ARSI), Rome.

order's first 'test of battle' (*pruova d'armi*) against the heresies of the age and, finally – Ignatius yet living – Africa together with the Spanish and Portuguese empires in the New World and East Indies saw the seeding of the Society's apostolate with the blood and sweat of its members.

This first volume of the history of the Society was also conceived from the outset as necessarily a polemic. As Bartoli put it, immediately after this passage, in his note to the reader:

> This History will count for me as two: i.e. not only as a History but also as an Apology. For there is no shortage of pens and tongues [belonging not only] to innumerable heretics but also to a great number of Catholics, who in a thousand ways, in both writing and speech, attempt to make the Society despised by the world and held in public contempt.[9]

It is therefore appropriate that in two major, recently published reference works about the Society, there are substantial entries and chapters devoted to anti-Jesuitism not only as a movement but also as a literary genre.[10] Already by 1564, eight years after Loyola's death, the Roman curialist and bishop Ascanio Cesarini had penned the pamphlet *Novi advertimenti*, which focused on the fact that the Society ignored the usual duties of religious orders by not singing or even saying their office in choir.[11] The lawyer Étienne Pasquier's *Le Catechisme des Jésuites* (1602) labelled the Jesuits as a 'hermaphrodite' order and accused them of being 'too little French', possessing 'two souls in their bodies. One Roman in Rome; the other French in France.'[12] Undoubtedly the longest-lasting of such works was, in fact, an example of *Jesuit* anti-Jesuitism: the *Monita secreta* (*Secret Instructions*), which claimed to contain secret advice that Jesuits gave to members in order to secure power, wealth and, ultimately, world domination. The author was an ex-Jesuit, Hieronim Zahorovsky, who came from Włodzimierz (in modern-day Ukraine), failed a theology exam and so was not admitted

---

[9] 'Varrammi ancora a doppio questa Historia; cioè non tanto per Historia, come per Apologia. Impercioche penne, e lingue non mancano, e d'heretici oltrenumero, e a gran numero di Catolici, che in mille form, scrivendo, e favellando, s'adoperan, secondo lor talento, per mettere in dispetto al mondo, e in publico vituperio la Compagnia ...' Second page of the 'A' Lettori' to *Della vita e dell'istituto di S. Ignatio fondatore della compagnia di Giesu libri cinque del P. Daniello Bartoli della Medesima Compagnia* (Rome, 1650). My sincere thanks to Franco D'Intino for assistance with translating Bartoli's baroque prose.

[10] 'Anti-Jesuit Polemic', in *Cambridge Encyclopedia of the Jesuits*, ed. Worcester, 30–5, and 'Anti-Jesuitism in a Global Perspective', in *Oxford Handbook of the Jesuits*, ed. Županov, 833–54.

[11] Sabina Pavone, 'The History of Anti-Jesuitism: National and Global Dimensions', in *The Jesuits and Globalization: Historical Legacies and Contemporary Challenges*, ed. Thomas Banchoff and José Casanova (Washington, DC, 2016), 111–30, at 112.

[12] Etienne Pasquier, *Le Catéchisme des Jésuites ou examen de leur doctrine*, ed. Claude Sutto (Québec, 1982), 186r. A modern English translation of this work, by Patricia M. Ranum and co-edited by Robert A. Maryks and Jotham Parsons, is forthcoming from Brill: *The Jesuits' Catechism or Their Doctrine Examined (1602)*.

to the ranks of those who took, in addition to the vows of chastity, poverty and obedience, a fourth vow of special service to the pope with regard to missions, and thereby was excluded from becoming a fully professed member of the Society.[13] The *Monita* was first printed in Kraków in 1614 and enjoyed an exceptionally long afterlife, being most recently reprinted in Moscow in 1996.[14]

To counter such works, in book 2 chapter 8 of his *Vita e dell'Istituto di S. Ignatio*, Bartoli urged the need for the Jesuits to be always on guard, as were the Israelites under Nehemiah when they rebuilt the walls of Jerusalem with one eye on their weapons nearby.[15] He then proceeded to list a long catalogue of the different kinds of works which had been written against the Jesuits, including poetry, history, novels, newsletters, trials, satires, philippics and prophecies – 'enough to fill a more than modest library', as he put it – to which the most effective antidote, in Bartoli's view, was Pedro de Ribabaneira's printed catalogue of works written by the Jesuits, of 1602, which had been revised and expanded by Philippe Alegambe in 1643.[16] This is the ancestor of Carlos Sommervogel's twelve-volume bibliography and its online successor.[17] This kind of reference work was not unique to the Jesuits – one thinks, for example, of Quétif and Echard's classic bibliography of Dominican authors, the *Scriptores ordinis praedicatorum* of 1719–21 – but the Society has, uniquely, kept up the tradition to the present day.

Bartoli in fact compared antipathy to the Society with the jealousy that the advent of such orders as the Dominicans and Franciscans had provoked in the thirteenth century, before listing a number of reasons (seven) why people might think badly of the Society.[18] These included ignorance; the reading of books such as the *Monita* (which amounted to the same thing); blaming the whole order just because there were bad apples; and the malignity of apostates. However, the real heavy lifting carried out by Bartoli's volume was done in demonstrating, first, the orthodoxy of Loyola's most important writing, the *Spiritual*

[13] My sincere thanks, once again, to Dr Flowers for putting me right on this other important detail.

[14] Sabina Pavone, *The Wily Jesuits and the 'Monita Secreta'. The Forged 'Secret Instructions' of the Jesuits: Myth and Reality* (St Louis, 2005). See appendix 2 of this book for a list of the numerous editions (both printed and manuscript), 234–42.

[15] Bartoli, *Della Vita e dell'Istituto di S. Ignatio*, 178.

[16] *Bibliotheca Scriptorum Societatis Iesu, post excusum anno MDCVIII. Catalogum R. P. Pietri Ribadeneirae Societatis Eiusdem Theologi, nunc hoc novo apparatu librorum ad annum reparatae salutis MDCXLII editorum concinnata et illustrium virorum elogiis adornata, Philippo Alegambe Bruxellensi ex eadem societate Iesu accedit Catalogus Religiosorum Societatis Iesu* (Antwerp, 1643).

[17] *Bibliothèque de la Compagnie de Jésus*, 2nd edn (12 vols., Brussels and Paris, 1890–1932); Jesuit Bibliography Online hosted by Boston College, Massachusetts: https://jesuitonline-bibliography.bc.edu.

[18] Bartoli, *Della Vita e dell'Istituto di S. Ignatio*, 186–207 (bk II, chs. 11–17).

*Exercises* – which essentially offers a programme for a month's silent retreat, including various techniques of prayer supplemented by approaches to discernment of the retreatant's own spiritual state and so was suspected of promoting the heresy of illuminism free of clerical control; secondly, the Society's distinctiveness in not reciting the office in choir (which was a particular target of Cesarini's early polemic); and, thirdly, why the Society possessed several grades of membership – fully professed priests (i.e. those who had taken the fourth vow of special obedience to the pope 'in regard to missions'), spiritual coadjutors (i.e. priested and therefore qualified to preach, teach and hear confession) and, finally, simple lay brothers, or, to give them their formal title, temporal coadjutors.[19] Those who belonged to this last grade, who also took vows of poverty, chastity and obedience, constituted, together with the spiritual coadjutors, between a quarter and a third of those in any single community.[20] Last but not least was Bartoli's emphasis on the significance of the fact that the first Jesuit companions had made their first vow of association on Montmartre and that martyrdom had subsequently become at once a symbol of the Society's legitimacy and a *lieu de mémoire* for subsequent historians and hagiographers of the order. Bartoli claimed that during the first century there had been at least 300 of his confreres who had lost their lives (the majority on the mission to Japan). His brief description leaves little to the imagination:

> [They were martyred] [b]y being slowly burned for two or three hours; drowned at sea; torn apart; sliced up; pierced with spears; crucified; beheaded; killed by immersion in freezing or boiling water; poisoned; hanged or [killed] by means of the cruellest Japanese torture of being suspended upside down over a ditch until all one's blood had slowly drained out from incisions made behind each ear.[21]

When reading such passages, we need to remember how, not only for the Jesuits, history was essentially a polemical and rhetorical exercise and remained subordinate to rhetoric, being a reservoir of *inventio*, that is to say, telling and memorable examples to drive home a point.[22] Moreover, as the art historian Helen Langdon has powerfully shown

---

[19] The grade of coadjutor is first mentioned in the revised *Formula of the Institute* of 1550. See *The Constitutions of the Society of Jesus and their Complementary Norms*, ed. John W. Padberg (St Louis, 1996), 3–13, at 5.

[20] Decree 82 para. 3 from the 6th General Congregation (1616), in *For Matters of Greater Moment: The First Thirty Jesuit General Congregations*, ed. J. Padberg, M. O'Keefe and J. McCarthy (St Louis, 1994), 275.

[21] Bartoli, *Della Vita e dell'Istituto di S. Ignatio*, 177.

[22] On the role of rhetoric in Bartoli's history of the Jesuits see Simon Ditchfield, 'The Limits of Erudition: Daniello Bartoli SJ (1608–1685) and the Mission of Writing History', in *Confessionalisation and Erudition in Early Modern Europe: An Episode in the History of the Humanities*, ed. Nicholas Hardy and Dmitri Levitin (Oxford, 2019), 218–39 (in particular, 227–32).

(and as I have argued elsewhere), Bartoli was the most visually aware of writers, a supreme ekphrasist, who provided direct inspiration for one of the most 'unorthodox and extravagant' painters of the Baroque, Salvator Rosa.[23]

## III

Generally speaking, the Jesuits wrote and argued better, and more often than not were better informed and prepared about the points at issue, than most of their opponents, Pascal and a very few others excepted. This was owing to the existence of a centralised information network of unprecedented scale and geographical scope as well as of an education programme, the famous *Ratio studiorum* (Method of Study), which though only finalised in 1599 had been trialled for an extended period beforehand and gave its students astonishing facility in the arts of persuasion (and in the process educated a sizeable proportion of the male offspring of the European elite of both Catholic and Protestant persuasion until the suppression of the Old Society in 1773).[24] Robert Maryks has calculated that students in the Jesuit colleges spent some five hours a day, 270 days of the year, in the company of classical, almost exclusively Latin, authors, pre-eminently Cicero, as a way of honing their skills.[25] Secondly, as we have seen, the Jesuits had plenty of opponents (including those within their own order), against whom to sharpen their quills. As Anthony Grafton taught us long ago (picking up on his teacher Arnaldo Momigliano's call to take notice of the contribution of antiquarians to the history of historical scholarship), polemic was a prodigious generator of erudition and scholarship in the age of humanism and of the Protestant and Catholic Reformations. Arguably, intra-Catholic squabbling had an even more profound and long-lasting impact.[26]

---

[23] Floriana Conte, *Tra Napoli e Milano. Viaggi di artisti nell'Italia del Seicento*, II. *Salvator Rosa* (Florence, 2014), 148–9; Helen Langdon, 'A Theatre of Marvels: The Poetics of Salvator Rosa', *Kunsthistorisk tidskrift*, 73 (2004), 179–92.

[24] Paul Nelles, 'Jesuit Letters', in *Oxford Handbook of the Jesuits*, ed. Županov, 44–72; *The Jesuit Ratio Studiorum: 400th Anniversary Perspectives*, ed. Vincent J. Duminuco (New York, 2000); Claude Pavur, *In the School of Ignatius: Studious Zeal and Devoted Learning* (Boston, MA, 2019). On the genesis and development of the *Ratio studiorum* see *Monumenta Paedagogica Societatis Iesu*, ed. L. Lukács (7 vols., Rome, 1965–92). The last three volumes contain the two full drafts from 1586, the 1591 draft as well as the 1599 one.

[25] Robert Maryks, *Saint Cicero and the Jesuits: The Influence of the Liberal Arts on the Adoption of Moral Probabilism* (Aldershot, 2008).

[26] Anthony Grafton, *Forgers and Critics: Creativity and Duplicity in Western Scholarship*, 2nd edn (Princeton, 2019); Arnaldo Momigliano, 'Ancient History and the Antiquarian', *Journal of the Warburg and Courthauld Institutes*, 13 (1950), 285–315. On intra-Catholic erudite squabbling and its implications see Simon Ditchfield, *Liturgy, Sanctity and History in Tridentine Italy: Pietro Maria Campi and the Preservation of the Particular* (Cambridge, 1995).

Another general point I want to make is the degree to which so many of our narratives and counter-narratives about the making of Roman Catholicism as a world religion have been shaped by the historiography authored by the religious orders. Again, this is not a new insight. In two of his four presidential addresses on 'Great Historical Enterprises', a former president of this society (1957–61), David Knowles, spoke eloquently of the contribution made by such great seventeenth-century scholars as his Benedictine forebear Jean Mabillon (1632–1707) to the science of diplomatics, and by the Jesuit Bollandists to textual scholarship in general as authors and editors of the most comprehensive collection of saints' lives ever undertaken, the multi-volume *Acta sanctorum* which began publication in Antwerp in 1642.[27] In the case of this last lecture, as an introduction to the Bollandists Knowles's sprightly account has never been bettered.

However, it is remarkable how many still treat such products of ecclesiastical erudition as mines of information rather than as rhetorical constructs. This is despite Luke Clossey's warning that we need to remember that Jesuit authors were not anthropologists *manqués*, but labourers in the vineyard of the Lord whose absolute priority was the saving of souls.[28] Moreover, the important work of such scholars as Ines Županov and Joan-Pau Rubiés has drawn attention to the varied purposes of the Jesuit 'art of describing' in Southeast and East Asia, and Pascale Girard's case study of accounts of Christian missions to China, the Philippines, Japan and Cochinchina has conclusively shown us that such histories are unavoidably textual constructs, which were subject not only to the constraints of genre and shaped by the expectations of their readers, but also written by authors who were not historians in the modern sense of the term, and so should not be read, naively, as 'protohistories' of the missions but rather as 'mythical' or at least symbolic narratives.[29]

In this regard, it is highly appropriate that the subject of this article, Daniello Bartoli, did not self-identify as an historian. Far from it, he referred to his multi-volume, though uncompleted, history of the Society, which he had only undertaken in 1648 at the specific behest of Vincenzo Carafa, the superior general, as 'this long and utterly tedious

---

[27] M. Knowles, 'Great Historical Enterprises, I. The Bollandists', *Transactions of the Royal Historical Society*, 8 (1958), 147–66; Knowles, 'Great Historical Enterprises II. The Maurists', *Transactions of the Royal Historical Society*, 9 (1959), 169–87.

[28] Luke Clossey, *Salvation and Globalization in the Early Jesuit Missions* (Cambridge, 2008), 8.

[29] Ines G. Županov, *Disputed Mission: Jesuit Experiments and Brahmanical Knowledge in 17th-Century India* (Oxford and New Delhi, 2001); Joan-Pau Rubiés, *Travellers and Cosmographers: Studies in the History of Early Modern Travel and Ethnology* (Aldershot, 2007); Pascale Girard, *Les religieux occidentaux en Chine à l'époque moderne: Essai d'analyse textuelle comparée* (Paris, 2000).

chore'.[30] A brief consideration of his career, on the one hand, and his published writings on the other, should help us to see not only where Bartoli was coming from but also the uses of history as he saw them. It is highly significant that he spent the first two decades of his career in the Society as a teacher, particularly of rhetoric, and then as a preacher. It was only after Bartoli's single adventure that even begins to compare with the trials and tribulations of so many of his missionary protagonists – his shipwreck off Capri – that the Jesuit is 'nailed [to his desk] in Rome' (*'inchiodato in Roma'*), to borrow his own turn of phrase, and told to set down the adventures of others at second hand (though he certainly put his direct experience of shipwreck to good use in his many descriptions of the storms endured by his brothers en route to Goa and the Far East).[31] It was only in his 'free time', so to speak, that he would be able to devote attention to writing treatises more to his taste.

Perhaps the most famous of these treatises in his lifetime, *The Man of Letters Defended and Emended*, published in 1645, a year before his shipwreck altered the trajectory of his career so dramatically, was something of a baroque bestseller, enjoying numerous Italian editions and translations – eight in the year of publication alone – and earning the approbation not only of that trophy Catholic convert and bluestocking Queen Christina of Sweden, but also of the artist Salvator Rosa to whom the (pirate) Florentine edition of the work of that year was dedicated by its printer.[32] This critical success serves to remind us that being a member of the Society of Jesus was far from incompatible with literary fashionability. The treatise argued for the virtues of solitude and the need for the true man of letters to cultivate *otium* and retreat from the life and business (*negotium*) of the court. Like those avatars of heroic freedom the ancient philosophers of antiquity such as Diogenes and Crates, who are presented by Bartoli in intensely visual language as 'astounding curiosities' who 'still live, still talk, still teach' by means of their sayings and actions, the man of letters should scorn earthly

---

[30] 'Quando piacerà a Dio ch'io la [Istoria] venga finita, applicherà l'animo e la penna a qualche libretto come soglio, per sollevamento dell'animo *da mia lunga e incredibilmente noiosa factica'* (emphasis added). From a letter from Bartoli to Giovanni Giacomo Brunelli, 15 July 1662. See *Lettere edite ed inedite dal padre Daniello Bartoli e di uomini illustri scritte al medesimo*, ed. G. Boero (Bologna, 1865), 31.

[31] Bartoli to Giovanni Giacomo Brunelli, 3 February 1657, in *Lettere edite ed inedite*, ed. Boero, 27.

[32] *Dell'Uomo di lettere difeso et emendato parti due* (Florence, 1645). Queen Christina asked to see a copy in Stockholm in the early 1650s even before she converted and travelled to Rome. See John J. Renaldo, *Daniello Bartoli, a letterato of the Seicento* (Naples, 1979), 71. Translations appeared in French (1651), German (1654), English (1660), Latin (1672) and Spanish (1678). There was also a belated Dutch translation (1722). See Daniello Bartoli, *The Man of Letters Defended and Amended*, ed. and trans. Gregory Woods (New York, 2018), vii–viii. I am most grateful to Dr Woods for sending me a copy of this valuable edition.

possessions and liberate himself from ambition and fear.[33] Here the world was a theatre of marvels, full of terrible beauty. Through his artful use of striking paradoxes – '*orrida bellezza*' (horrible beauty) is just one of many – and arresting visual language, Bartoli unsettled his audience's perception of the world, thereby provoking awareness of its deeper, underlying unity.

Moreover, it was a world in which geography was to be considered as complementary to history, in the same way that the tongue (history) let the eyes (geography) speak.[34] Without geography the earth was but a dark planet since one did not know where events were taking place.[35] As a sometime pupil of the astronomer and natural philosopher Ricciotti, we should not be surprised at Bartoli's interest in the natural world not simply as a source of metaphors, for he was also the author of several scientific treatises. One of these, on atmospheric pressure, referred to the debate between Robert Boyle and others over the existence of the vacuum.[36] In this treatise Bartoli was concerned, above all, with not compromising the orthodox, Aristotelian position which denied the possibility of the vacuum. Throughout, he was content to cite the experiments of others (though we know he owned a copy of Boyle's works and disagreed with them).[37] The other two treatises dedicated specifically to natural history were on acoustics and on the freezing properties of water.[38] According to John Renaldo, Bartoli's three scientific treatises which, as we have just seen, were devoted to ice (touch), the vacuum (sight) and to sound (hearing), were part of a single project to attack those, such as Boyle, who concluded that empirical method proved the existence of atoms and thereby subordinated reason to cognition:

> By the last half of the Seicento the role of right reason in the conversion of non-Christians served as the basis for much of the Society's missionary role. In the case of the Chinese particularly, the Jesuits argued in their official histories of the mission

---

[33] Helen Langdon, 'Philosophy and Magic', in H. Langdon with X. Solomon and C. Volpi, *Salvator Rosa* (London, 2010), 194–201, at 195–6.

[34] 'Cieca dunque è l'Istoria, se a veder la terra le manca il lume della Geografia. Altresì la Geografia, se l'historia non le dà che parlare, da sè sola è mutola'. Bartoli, *La Geografia trasportata al Morale* (Rome, 1664), but consulted here in the collected edition of his moral treatises: *Delle Opere del P. Daniello Bartoli, della Compagnia del Giesu, Le Morali* (Rome, 1684), 392.

[35] 'E quanto all'Istoria, ella, senza la Geografia è come orba; così tutta al buio on sa a qual parte della terra si volgere per rinvendire il dove de' fatti, che suo mestiere è fare palese al mondo; e convenevole collocar giustamente ogni cosa a'suoi luoghi.' Bartoli, *Delle Opere ... Le Morali*, 391.

[36] *La Tensione e la Pressione disputanti qual di loro sostenga l'argento vivo ne, cannelli dopo fattone il vuoto. Discorso del P. Daniello Bartoli della Compagnia di Giesu* (Bologna, 1677).

[37] I am indebted to Antonio Clericuzio of the University of Roma Tre for discussion with me on this point.

[38] *Del suono, de' tremori armonici e dell'udito* (Bologna, 1680); *Del ghiaccio e della coagulazione* (Rome, 1681).

that right reason had brought the Chinese to the very portals of the Church. If man did truly learn only through experience, and Christianity was the result of the experience of the Latin west, then the Christian tradition would be significantly limited. In fact missionary activity on all levels, and not just in China, would be rendered fruitless if not foolish.[39]

Ultimately, for Bartoli, atomism threatened to break the chain of God's creation by discouraging curiosity about the natural world, which, for the Jesuit, was all about linking parts to the whole. As he put it in his treatise on ice:

> The world is nothing more than one great machine composed of many smaller machines so closely linked together that they work perfectly. Each of these smaller machines is composed of so many small parts, all of such a nature and working in such a way that their operation should not arouse in you curiosity about their particular nature but should rather elevate your mind to an act of philosophical wonder.[40]

## IV

So far so (relatively) straightforward it would appear. Here we have Bartoli the experienced teacher and preacher (with hinterland) who was commanded to write a history of the Society in a period when history was still seen, not as an autonomous discipline, but rather as a reservoir of stirring and striking examples to praise the good and damn the bad. This logic becomes even clearer when one takes into account that from its very beginnings the Society had been constituted in such a way as to ensure that not only would Bartoli's rhetorical talents be matched closely to the task at hand but he would be furnished with plenty of raw material through membership of a religious order for which the effective circulation of information was its lifeblood. To begin with, there was a stress from the outset on the importance of instilling into new members of the Society a sense of the order's history. Already by 1565 the Second General Congregation of the Society specified in a single decree concerning 'the manner of communicating' not only the frequency with which local superiors should write to their provincials but when both of them should write to the superior general.[41]

The *Constitutions* of the Society, published in 1558, only two years after the founder's death, required superiors of individual Jesuit houses to write weekly to their provincial who, in turn, was obliged to write to the superior general, also on a weekly basis if close, and monthly if located at a greater distance from Rome. The key figure here, and

[39] John J. Renaldo, 'Bacon's Empiricism, Boyle's Science, and the Jesuit Response in Italy', *Journal of the History of Ideas*, 37 (1976), 689–95, at 691.

[40] Bartoli, *Del ghiaccio*, 47 as translated in ibid., 693. I propose to discuss in greater detail in a forthcoming study the ways in which Bartoli's science informed his history writing.

[41] *For Matters of Greater Moment*, 124–5 (decree 54).

arguably second only to Loyola himself in shaping the Society's DNA, was Juan Alfonso de Polanco, who acted as secretary of the Society for no fewer than twenty-six years from 1547.[42] For Polanco the letter was the law, in a very real sense, and although the level of frequency just mentioned was soon abandoned as impracticable, a Jesuit letter-writing manual of 1620 refers to at least sixteen different kinds of documents which provincials were obliged to send to Rome on a regular basis, as Markus Friedrich has noted in his important work on Jesuit governance.[43] The resulting archive offers scholars to this day the opportunity to gauge the grasp as well as measure the reach of an institution which is only comparable to the archives of the papacy itself in its claim to command a genuinely global frame of reference.[44] Furthermore, rectors of colleges were instructed to prepare annual catalogues of those resident, to send to their provincials who would then send them on to the superior general. These catalogues are still held in the Jesuit archive in Rome, and the more detailed ones, compiled every three years (*catalogi triennales*), enable us to know the number, age, origins, education, date of final vows (if applicable), state of health and ministries performed by each member of a community.[45] In a further, 'secret catalogue' (*catalogus secretus*) the human qualities of each member of the community were set down according to the following instructions:

> Skills and qualities of each one should be described in the second catalogue, that is: talent, judgment, practical wisdom, practical experience, advancement in arts, physical appearance, and particular skills for performing the Society's ministries.[46]

[42] Nelles, 'Jesuit Letters'.

[43] *Constitutions of the Society of Jesus*, paras. 673–6 (pp. 326 and 328). See also M. Friedrich, 'Communication and Bureaucracy in the Early Modern Society of Jesus', *Schweizerische Zeitschrift für Religions- und Kulturgeschichte*, 101 (2007), 49–75, at 56; and Friedrich, *Der lange Arm Roms? Globale Verwaltung und Kommunikation im Jesuitenorden, 1540–1773* (Frankfurt and New York, 2011).

[44] Although the date of foundation of the Vatican Apostolic Archive (AAV), formerly known as the Vatican Secret Archive (ASV), is traditionally given as 1612, no attempt was made to create a complete index until that of Giuseppe Garampi who as prefect of the archive (1751–72) oversaw the creation of the famous 'Schedario Garampi', which he considered as a first stage in the writing of a genuinely global history of the Roman Church, entitled *Orbis christianus*. It consists of 800,000 index cards, which were stuck into 125 folio volumes in the nineteenth century and are still in daily use by scholars with the assistance of *Sussidi per la consultazione dell'Archivio Vaticano. Lo schedario Garampi – i registri vaticani – i registri lateranensi – le 'rationes camerae' – l'archivio consistoriale*, new edn, ed. G. Gualdo (Vatican City: Archivio segreto, 1989), part 1.

[45] E. Lamalle, 'Les catalogues des provinces et des domiciles de la Compagnie de Jésus', *Archivum Historicum Societatis Iesu*, 13 (1944), 77–101.

[46] 'In secundo catalogo dotes et qualitates uniuscuiusque describantur, videlicet: ingenium, iudicium, prudentia, experientia rerum, profectus in litteris, naturalis complexio, et ad quae Societatis ministeria talentum habeat.' *Institutum Societatis Iesu* (3 vols., Florence, 1892–3), III, 45.

According to Cristiano Casalini, although catalogues of individual members had been kept by the Benedictines, the Franciscans and Dominicans, such a systematic attempt at personality profiling, based on the assumption that the body and soul were connected, was new. It was also consonant with Ignatian spirituality, since the *Spiritual Exercises*, in the words of Casalini, 'affirmed the idea of psychosomatic unity as the fundamental lens through which to examine the individual'.[47] Although the physician-philosopher Galen (129–*c*.216 CE) had bequeathed to the West (via Arabic) the doctrine of the four humours – blood, phlegm, yellow and black bile – to explain temperament, it was left to the Spaniard Juan Huarte de San Juan, in his treatise *Examen de ingenios* ('Examination of talents') of 1575, to argue how these humours also determined an individual's particular skills, and to the Jesuits to adopt the doctrine wholesale, as reflected not only in their catalogues but also in their rules for study, the *Ratio studiorum* (1599).

Here is the relevant information about Bartoli which was collected for one such entry into the triennial catalogue dating from 1633, when he was just twenty-five and living and working in the prestigious Jesuit college in Parma, which enjoyed particularly generous support from the ruling Farnese dynasty. Going from left to right, it judges Bartoli according to the following qualities: first, *Ingenium* (intellectual capabilities) – 'Bonum'; second, *Iudicium* (judgement) – 'Bonum'; third, *Prudentia* (prudence) – 'Moderate'; fourth, *Experientia reru[m]* (life experience) – 'Esigua' (Limited); fifth, *Profectus in litteris* (educational capabilities) – 'Optimus [in the] Hum[anitates]'; sixth, *Naturalis complexio* (temperament) – 'Melancholia'; and finally, seventh, *Aptus ad omnia fere societatis ministeria* – he has aptitude for almost all ministries/duties/roles in the Society (Figure 3).

Given the apparent breadth of Bartoli's intellectual capabilities, it can perhaps be of little surprise that no fewer than five attempts to be sent on missions 'to the Indies' were declined. Bartoli was one of the many who wrote to the father general seeking to be sent to the Indies; there are over 14,000 such letters extant dating from before the suppression of the Society in 1773, whose writers were disappointed. Bartoli's potential as teacher, preacher, writer and administrator was clearly regarded as being too valuable to let him be sent overseas, where the mortality rate on the voyage from Lisbon to Goa could be as high as 50 per cent.[48]

---

[47] For this and what follows see C. Casalini, 'Discerning Skills: Psychological Insight at the Core of Jesuit Identity', in R. Maryks, *Exploring Jesuit Distinctiveness: Interdisciplinary Perspectives on Ways of Proceeding within the Society of Jesus* (Leiden and Boston, MA, 2016), 189–211.

[48] Five letters addressed from Bartoli to the Superior General Muzio Vitelleschi (1563–1645) survive from a seven-year period (February 1627 to October 1635): ARSI, *F.G. 738*,

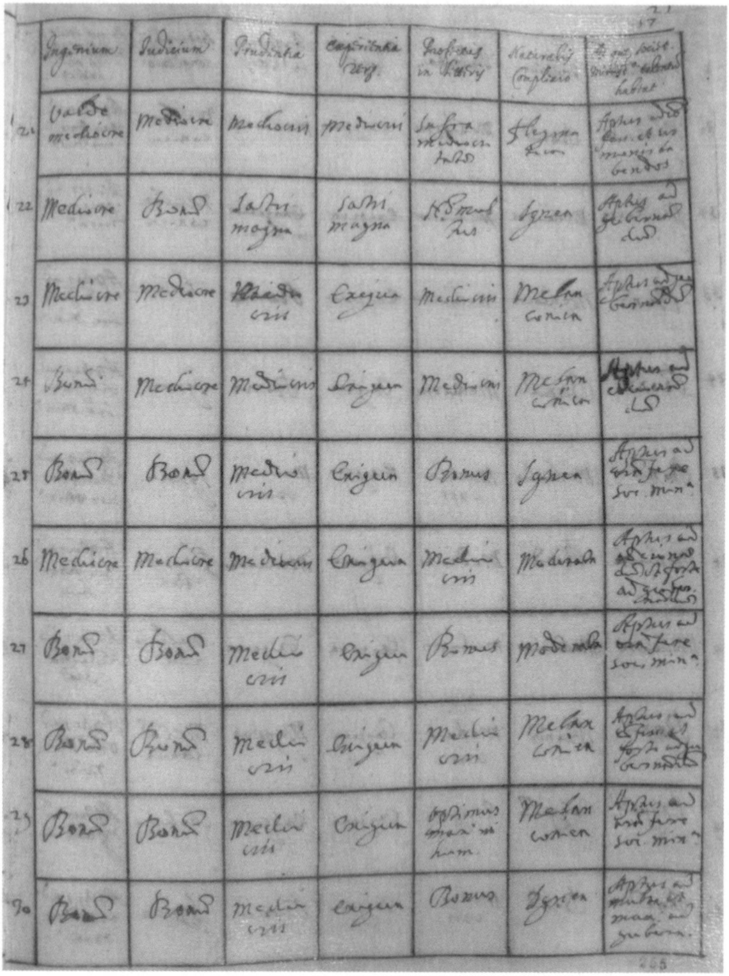

Figure 3. Archivum Historicum Societatis Iesu (ARSI), Ven. 391, fol. 255r. Bartoli is the penultimate listed, number 29. Image courtesy of ARSI.

fols. 7r and 189r; *F.G. 739*, fols. 179r and 239r; *F.G. 740*, fol. 363r. These have been printed in *Lettere edite ed inedite*, ed. Boero, 1–7. Unusually, we also have Vitelleschi's replies, which have been printed in *Lettere edite ed inedite*, 81–3. For the mortality rate on board ship from Lisbon to Goa see L. Brockey, *Journey to the East: The Jesuit mission to China, 1579–1724* (Cambridge, MA, and London, 2007), 37.

It is within this context that we need to interpret the insistence of the founders of the Jesuits from the outset not only on the importance of history to the Society's very identity but also on the desirability of knowledge about the foreign cultures encountered by its members on overseas mission. This is laid out by the *Constitutions*:

> Sufficient information about the Society should be given to them [those admitted to probation] at this time, *both by direct conversation and from a study of its history*, as also from its principal documents both older ones (such as the *Formula* of the Institute, the *General Examen* and the *Constitutions* or experts from them) and more recent ones [*Norms*, 25 §4] ... Those who are in charge of formation should take care that our members, especially in the period immediately after the novitiate, *become familiar with the sources of the spirituality of the Church and the Society, with its history and traditions*, and that they study them with a view toward their own progress and the progress of others. [Norms, 69 §1] (Emphasis added)[49]

Although the composition of the *Constitutions* was complete by the time of Loyola's death in 1556 (having undergone three successive stages in 1547, 1550 and 1553) and received papal approval in 1558, they only took on a more complete form in 1635, when the initial framework was published together with explanatory glosses and norms in a volume called the Institute of the Society of Jesus (*Institutum Societatis Iesu*), a document which was updated several times in the eighteenth and nineteenth centuries.[50] I draw your attention particularly to the fact that members of the Society were expected to internalise their sense of history *from conversation* as well as study, which reminds us that just as their prowess in Ciceronian Latin was a spoken skill so was their capacity to debate and argue essentially *oral*. Works such as Bartoli's *Istoria* were to be *heard* and not just read.[51] As Jennifer Richards has rightly insisted, we must *learn to listen* to early modern texts and, as scholars, be much more voice-aware. The Age of Print did not silence the written word. Rather it 'aligned eye, tongue and ear' and 'allowed oral literacy to flourish' as never before.[52]

---

[49] *Constitutions of the Society of Jesus*, 75, 145.

[50] My understanding of the development of the Constitutions and their relationship with the Institutum derives from Markus Friedrich, 'Jesuit Organization and Legislation: Development and Implementation of a Normative Framework', in *Oxford Handbook of the Jesuits*, ed. Županov, 23–43, at 24–7.

[51] See, for example, the letter of Bartoli to Giovanni Girolamo Brunelli (30 December 1651), in which the Jesuit refers to: 'la Vita di Sant'Ignazio, che m'hanno onorato di leggere in pubblico'. *Lettere edite ed inedite*, ed. Boero, 13.

[52] Jennifer Richards, *Voices and Books in the English Renaissance: A New History of Reading* (Oxford, 2019), 10.

# V

The second volume of Bartoli's *Istoria*, after that on the Society's founder, was published a few years after the life of St Ignatius, in 1653. It was dedicated to Asia, and the first four of its eight books were almost entirely given over to the figure who, not only in Bartoli's eyes, was seen in many ways as the co-founder of the Society, the Basque nobleman Francis Xavier, and his missions to India, the Moluccas and Japan. Bartoli availed himself extensively of the resources available to him in Rome courtesy of the Jesuit habits of record-keeping, as first Josef Wicki and now Elisa Frei have shown in their exhaustive editorial work which one can consult in the latest edition, based on that of 1667.[53] However, in fact 'the Dante of baroque prose', as the major romantic poet and essayist Giacomo Leopardi (1798–1837) later called Bartoli, was true to this epithet and made extensive use of such sources as the numerous letters and testimonies of witnesses from Xavier's beatification and canonisation trials (including the all-important summary reports made on behalf of the auditors of the Rota, the highest papal court) as raw material for his own artful elaborations.[54]

Again and again, Bartoli can be seen to prefer narrative sources over archival ones; not because he did not value the latter, but simply because his purpose was different. He set this out in a very brief, undated document, probably written around the time of the composition of the volume on Asia.[55] This is the closest we can get to knowing for sure what he thought he was doing and is entitled simply: 'How to write the history of the Society'. This two-sided document includes such statements as the following: 'If we are to do justice to the subject; one needs to break free of Chronology … in order to consider a mission, a life, a persecution [without breaking the narrative thread] … For this one needs to arrange the history according to place [geographically rather than rhetorically speaking].' Bartoli explicitly distinguished his approach from the scrupulously chronological one which, as has already been seen, had been undertaken by Niccolò Orlandini and Francesco Sacchini and was being continued by Pierre Poussine. Bartoli noted how all three

[53] Daniello Bartoli, *Istoria della Compagnia di Gesù. L'Asia*, ed. Umberto Grassi and Elisa Frei (2 vols., Turin, 2019); Josef Wicki, 'Vorarbeiten für eine geplante kritische Ausgabe der Asia des P.D. Bartoli SJ', *Aufsätze zur portugeisischen Kulturgeschichte*, 18 (1983), 202–43; Wicki, 'L'Asia I, libro 7 sull'India (1553–1572)', in *Daniello Bartoli storico e letterato* (Ferrara, 1986), 17–30.

[54] Bartoli, *L'Asia*, vol. 1, e.g. 11, 33, 341, 423–4, 461, 501.

[55] 'Del modo di scrivere l'istoria della Compagnia, manoscritto autografo di Daniello Bartoli', ARSI, *Epp. NN. 96*, fols. 18r–19v. A full transcription, translation and commentary of this important document is currently in preparation. The only published version, by Maria Brutto Barone Adesi ('Daniello Bartoli storico', *Rivista di storia di storiografia*, 1 (1980), 77–102) is unreliable and misleading. My thanks to Elisa Frei for her transcription.

took full advantage of the steady stream of letters, above all the quarterly ones which arrived regularly at the Jesuit headquarters in Rome, from outside Europe. He also noted how these authors all wrote chronology, not history, sacrificing thereby the coherence of events to the sequence of time and, in the process, fragmenting the narrative into tiny pieces. As Bartoli concluded: 'What seems to me to be novel, and for this reason worth doing, is that there is no other religious order where one can begin with its origins ... and then go on to offer histories of the four parts of the world ...'[56]

So, for Bartoli, while there are numerous references to letters in his history, they performed another function that was not just about their content but their importance to the story being told; firstly to the prot- agonists themselves and then to their audiences in the Old World. To limit myself to his volume on Asia, Xavier was not just a writer of letters but a grateful receiver of them. Basing himself, in part, on one of Xavier's own letters, Bartoli notes how the missionary saint read and reread those he received from his brothers in Europe, before kissing them a thousand times, and soaking them with his tears as he recalled those who had sent them.[57] He even cut out the signatures from the letters and wore them, as if they were relics, around his neck.[58] On another occasion, Bartoli mentioned that on his travels Xavier carried just three things with him, around his neck, which were collected together like a reliquary. They were a bone fragment belonging to the Apostle to Asian Christianity, St Thomas; an autograph signature of Ignatius Loyola; and Xavier's profession of faith written in his own hand.[59] Elsewhere, on several occasions, Bartoli referred to the consolation which letters with their tales of missionary derring-do gave to their confreres in Europe who were also experiencing difficulties.[60]

## VI

Turning to Bartoli's treatment of the Jesuit mission to Japan, which appeared in 1660, ten years after his first volume on Ignatius but after

[56] 'Che se ciò sembra nuovo, nuova ancor'è la cagione di farlo; non vi essendo altra Religione che possa cominciare da suoi principii ... historie che per le quattro parti del mondo come la Compagnia'. ARSI, *Epp. NN. 96*, fol. 19v.

[57] Bartoli, *L'Asia*, vol. I, 136–7; *The Letters and Instructions of Francis Xavier*, trans. and ed. M. Joseph Costelloe (St Louis, 1992), 130.

[58] 'A quante lettere gli scrivevano i nostri da Europa e dall'India, tagliava i nomi delle sottoscrizioni, a portavali al collo, come reliquie di santi uomini, e come dolci memorie da consolarsi.' Bartoli, *L'Asia*, vol. I, 533.

[59] '... un minuzzolo d'osso dell'apostolo S. Tomaso primo padre della cristianità orien- tale; uno sottoscrizione del santo padre Ignazio... e la sua professione religiosa, scritta di proprio pugno'. Bartoli, *L'Asia*, vol. I, 534.

[60] Bartoli, *L'Asia*, vol. II, 137–8, 154, 228.

only two of the three editions of that on Asia which were published in 1653, 1656 and 1667 (the last of these incorporating a new section on the Mission to the Mughal emperor Akbar, which had been separately published in 1663), the historian had already described Japan extensively as the background to Xavier's mission of 1549–51 in book 3 of Asia. He was careful also to emphasise the correspondences which he believed existed between Japanese and Christian society. In particular, he followed the widespread tendency in European accounts of the time to project onto the Japanese a 'religion' which was identifiably 'Western', with its parallel hierarchy, monasteries, monks, temples, processions and sacred books. In this he was of course following, albeit in a more attenuated fashion, one of the very earliest reports about Japanese religion given by the French linguist and mystic Guillaume Postel in his *Des mervailles du Monde* of 1553, in which the French scholar argued that 'the Japanese were basically Christians, albeit ones who had forgotten much of the True Gospels'.[61] As it happened, the Japanese, in their own way, returned the compliment by regarding Christianity as deformed Buddhism; a supposition which appeared to be confirmed by the fact that the missionaries also came from India, which had been the source of Buddhist teachings almost precisely a thousand years before. However, as Joan-Pau Rubiés has shown in his subtle and searching analysis of the so-called Yamaguchi disputations of September 1551 between Xavier together with some of his fellow missionaries and some Buddhist monks, one is speaking of a dialogue only in the sense of finding some common ground for disagreement.[62] Moreover, in the course of the conversations, the Sorbonne-trained Xavier was careful *not* to analyse the diversity within Buddhism as in any way analogous to the diversity within Latin Christendom.

For a broader context, one needs also to bear in mind that between 1598 and 1650 no fewer than ninety-one martyrological works on Japan had been published in Western Europe (including two plays by Lope da Vega), so that Bartoli had precedent when he moved on to write his volume of the history of the Society in England after those on Japan (1660) and China (1663).[63] The second part of Pedro de Ribadeneira's immensely popular *Historia ecclesiastica del cisma del Reino di Inglaterra* had explicitly juxtaposed the flourishing state of Japanese

[61] J. Ānanda Josephson, *The Invention of Religion in Japan* (Chicago, 2012), 59.

[62] J.-P. Rubiés, 'Real and Imaginary Dialogues in the Jesuit Mission of Sixteenth-Century Japan', *Journal of the Economic and Social History of the Orient*, 55 (2012), 447–94.

[63] Rady Roldán-Figueroa, *The Martyrs of Japan: Publication History and Catholic Missions in the Spanish World (Spain, New Spain, and the Philippines, 1597–1700)* (Leiden, 2021). See also Rady Roldán-Figueroa, 'Father Luis Piñeiro, S.J., the Tridentine Economy of Relics, and the Defense of the Jesuit Missionary Enterprise in Tokugawa Japan', *Archiv für Reformationsgeschichte/Archive for Reformation History*, 101 (2010), 207–30.

Christianity with the deplorable state of that in England as early as 1593; a comparison which likely provoked Bartoli to refer to England, in a letter, as 'Europe's Japan'.[64] Bartoli began, literally, at the beginning, with his account of how the Japanese themselves described the beginning of the world – their Genesis story, if you like. He went on to describe its geography and its climate, which he reported was similar to that of Sicily though much windier, before giving what was overall an unambiguously positive assessment of the Japanese people. He admired Japanese eloquence and emphasised their fierce code of honour. Compared with the Christian converts in India, the Japanese were, on the whole, much more constant and indeed tenacious in their new faith. Indeed, Bartoli never lost the opportunity to emphasise the nobility in both spirit and blood of the Japanese martyrs, both young and old. This detail alone strongly suggests that the audience was intended to be the noble pupils attending Jesuit colleges; the same students who would also take part in the famous Latin plays, many of which were on subjects taken from the most heroic, early-Christian period of history. The longest two entries in the index to the first edition of *Giappone* are on 'Japanese women memorable for their virtue' (their Christian names constitute a veritable roll call of early Christian heroines: Massentia, Marta, Tecla, Susanna, Monica, etc.) and on 'Extraordinary torments given to [Japanese] Christians'. The list of tortures, which ran to one and a half columns, left little to the imagination, and the sufferings of several Japanese martyrs made their way back to Europe in such works as Matthaeus Tanner's martyrology of the Society.[65] Bartoli's narrative ends with the expulsion of the Jesuit missionaries more or less one hundred years after Xavier's arrival.

## VII

This is more or less the chronological end point too of Bartoli's third part of the Asian mission, and the next to be published, in 1663, on China.[66] If the volume on Japan came to resemble a contemporary updating of the Roman martyrology, with its mainly Japanese together with a few Jesuit martyrs standing in for their late antique prototypes, and successive

[64] Pedro de Ribadeneyra, *Segunda parte de la historia ecclesiastica del scisma de Inglaterra* (Alcalá de Henares, 1593), bk III, ch. 20; Letter to Giovanni Giacomo Brunelli, 9 June 1665, in *Lettere edite ed inedite*, ed. Boero, 32–3. There is now an English translation and critical edition by Spencer J. Weinreich: *Pedro de Ribadeneyra's 'Ecclesiastical History of the Schism of the Kingdom of England': A Spanish Jesuit's History of the English Reformation* (Leiden, 2017).

[65] Matthäus Tanner, *Societatis Iesu, usque ad sanguinis et vitae profusionem in Europa, Africa, Asia et America contra gentiles, mahometanos, judaeos, haereticos, impios pro Deo Fide Ecclesia pietate* (Prague, 1675), 207–432 (for Jesuit martyred in Asia).

[66] Bartoli, *Dell'historia della Compagnia di Giesu. La Cina. Terza parte dell'Asia* (Rome, 1663).

shoguns for pagan Roman emperors, Bartoli's narrative on the Jesuits in China was very different. Notwithstanding the chaos that accompanied the transition from the Ming to Qing dynasties in the middle decades of the seventeenth century, which during the final years of the regency of the Kangxi emperor (reigned 1661–1722) had effectively led to the Jesuits being under house arrest, Bartoli's tale was upbeat – and indeed by the end of the 1660s the fortunes of the Society were to be spectacularly reversed when the Flemish astronomer and mathematician Ferdinand Verbiest (1623–1688) was able to take advantage of the opportunity given to him by the young emperor to demonstrate the superiority of Western astronomy over its Chinese counterpart to be appointed director of the Imperial Mathematical Tribunal and become sometime tutor to the longest-serving and arguably most successful ruler in Chinese history. However, this postdated Bartoli's account, which instead focused on the success of Matteo Ricci's mission.

This focus was for the very obvious reason that Bartoli had by his side Ricci's account of his time in China, which was only publicly available then in a Latin rendition, published in 1615, that had been translated out of the vernacular by the Flemish Jesuit Nicolas Trigault and used by him to help raise money, very successfully as it turned out, for the Chinese mission. However, on several occasions in his text, Bartoli insists on the fact that Ricci, not Trigault, was the true author of this text, which remained unpublished until the twentieth century.[67] As is well enough known, the account of the Jesuit mission to China as mediated by Matteo Ricci is one of hard work mastering the Confucian classics and the art of Chinese composition, and small setbacks mostly orchestrated by imperial officials jealous of the Jesuit's talents. It reached a fitting conclusion with Ricci's transformation into a silk-clad honorary member of the Chinese literary elite, known as Li Madou, and his burial consisting, at the emperor's insistence, of an uneasy marriage of Confucian and Christian rituals.[68]

In this volume, Bartoli gave free rein to his interest in geography and astronomy, describing in some detail not only the enormous size of the Chinese empire, but also its corresponding wealth and the sophistication of its mandarin elite. Bartoli's admiration centred on the figure of Confucius, whose ethical teachings and their focus on ceremony, obedience and order sustained a European-wide Sinophilia until at least the

[67] For an excellent discussion of Trigault's 'curated' translation and its purpose see Nicholas Lewis, 'Revisiting *De Christiana Expeditione* as an Artefact of Globalisation', *Itinerario*, 45 (2021), 47–69.

[68] Nicholas Standaert, *The Interweaving of Rituals: Funerals in the Cultural Exchange between China and Europe* (Seattle, 2008), *ad indicem*.

mid-eighteenth century. The only fault that Bartoli could see in the Chinese was their ignorance that there was anything worth knowing outside their vast realm: which was why Ricci's diplomatic success in showing the emperor his map of the world without provoking imperial fury is surely the high point in his account. Given Bartoli's own interest in scientific instruments, clearly visible in his frequent deployment of astronomical metaphors, and his interest in navigation displayed particularly in his first volume on the missions in Asia (which may have its origins in the fact, as has been noted, that he had been a colleague of the astronomer Giovanni Battista Riccioli in Bologna), it is strange that so little was made of the role played by these skills in securing imperial favour for the Jesuits in China. There is, for example, no reference whatsoever to the German Jesuit, Adam Schall von Bell (1599–1666), who oversaw modification of the Chinese calendar under the last Ming emperor and also skilfully managed to ingratiate himself with the founder of the Qing dynasty, the Shunzhi emperor, who made him director of the Imperial Observatory.

## VIII

The final two volumes of Bartoli's history of the Society were on Europe – England (1667) and Italy (1673). He does not appear even to have begun to work on collecting material for the volume which had been envisaged on the Americas. I have already analysed the volume on England at some length elsewhere; suffice it to say here that it was very different from all the others in two respects: first, its deployment of many more primary documents and, second, its tight focus on proving the compatibility of loyalty to the papacy with loyalty to the English crown.[69] Accordingly, it concentrated overwhelmingly on the reign of Queen Elizabeth and the heroic martyrdom of several Jesuit missionaries, most famously Edmund Campion (1540–1581). The volume on Italy was scarcely less polemical and defensive, although the focus here was on the doctrinal orthodoxy of the Jesuits. Much space was given to their contribution to the deliberations of the Council of Trent including, crucially, the discussions which specifically related to Justification. Attention was also paid to the positive contribution made by the Society by means of their schools and colleges as well as their missions to the 'Other Indies'; that is to say, the backwoods bereft of adequate religious instruction, where priests were dressed no differently from their peasant parishioners with whom they worked side-by-side in the fields to support their wives and children. Bartoli's example here is Silvestro Landini's mission to

---

[69] Ditchfield, 'Limits of Erudition', 233–7.

Corsica, which the Jesuit famously compared to India in a letter to Loyola.[70] As with the volume on England, that on Italy also had a narrow chronological focus: beginning with Loyola's arrival at the gates of Rome in 1537 and ending with the election of Francisco Borja as superior general in 1565.

A much better-known treatment than Bartoli's of the Jesuits as missionaries to all four parts of the world, with which I draw this article to a close, is Andrea Pozzo's dizzying fresco, 'The worldwide mission of the Society of Jesus'. This covered the enormous nave ceiling of S. Ignazio in Rome, a church that was physically integrated into what remained the largest education complex in Western Europe until the nineteenth century, the Collegio Romano in central Rome. The church of S. Ignazio's prominent role in the ceremonial and liturgical life of the students at the Society's pre-eminent educational establishment made it even more central to the daily routine of the many future Jesuit missionaries who studied or taught there than the Society's mother church located less than 500 metres away. Pozzo, who was incidentally a temporal coadjutor, i.e. a lay brother in the Society, and so would likely have been very familiar with Bartoli's narrative from countless communal meals in the refectory, carried out work on the fresco between 1691 and 1694, in the decade after the writer's death. This image will likely be known even to those readers who don't work on either the Jesuits or the Protestant or Catholic Reformations, since it has become the 'go-to' image for any publisher, author or lecturer who wants a striking image to stand for the making of Roman Catholicism as a world religion in the early modern period. Indeed, Pozzo described it himself in the following terms:

> My idea in the painting was to represent the works of St Ignatius and of the Company of Jesus in spreading the Christian faith worldwide. In the first place, I embraced the entire vault with a building depicted in perspective. Then in the middle of this I painted the three persons of the Trinity; from the breast of one of which, that is the Human Son, issue forth rays that wound the heart of St Ignatius, and from him they issue, as a reflection spread to the four parts of the world depicted in the guize of Amazons … These torches that you see in the two extremities of the vault represent the zeal of St Ignatius – who in sending his companions to preach the Gospel said to them: 'Go and set the world alight (*Ite, incendite, infiammate omnia*), verifying in him Christ's words (Luke 12:49): 'I am come to send fire on the earth; and what will I but that it be kindled? (*Ignem veni mittere in terram, et quid volo nisi ut accendatur*).'[71]

[70] Bartoli, *Dell'Istoria della Compagnia di Giesu. L'Italia. Prima parte del Europa* (Rome, 1673), 255–9.

[71] Evonne Levy, *Propaganda and the Jesuit Baroque* (Berkeley and Los Angeles, 2004), 151. Pozzo's explanation may be found in the pamphlet *Breve descrittione della pittura fatta nella volta del tempio di Sant'Ignazio scoperta l'anno MDCXCIV per la festa del medesimo santo* (Rome, 1694), which can be viewed at https://archive.org/stream/brevedescrittionookoma#-page/2/mode/2up, last accessed 2 April 2021. My thanks to Professor Levy for directing

I hope that this article has managed to convince the reader that even if they cannot disagree with Pascal, they can agree that Bartoli's equally polemical, if more various, word-painting has been at least worth the detour. It was apparently said of Bill Haley and the Comets' famous hit record, '(We're Gonna) Rock around the Clock', first issued in 1954, and which inspired this article's title, that it could subsequently be heard playing on jukeboxes in the four corners of the globe.[72] I am sure that Bartoli would not have been displeased with such a comparison: *Bartolum sonant.*

me to the location of this very rare pamphlet. Save for the biblical passage, which is taken from *The Vulgate Bible*, 6: *The New Testament, Douay–Rheims Translation* (Cambridge, MA, and London, 2013), 389, the translation is Levy's.

[72] Although, arguably, this only happened some two decades later when the song opened the double LP of the soundtrack to the film *American Graffiti* (1973).

*Transactions of the RHS* 31 (2021), pp. 75–88 © The Author(s), 2021. Published by Cambridge University Press on behalf of the Royal Historical Society
doi:10.1017/S0080440121000049

# WHAT HAPPENS WHEN A WRITTEN CONSTITUTION IS PRINTED? A HISTORY ACROSS BOUNDARIES

## *The Prothero Lecture*

### By Linda Colley

READ 8 DECEMBER 2020

ABSTRACT. After 1750, the rate at which new political constitutions were generated increased relentlessly. By the First World War, written and published devices of this sort already operated in parts of every continent outside Antarctica. Yet for all the scale and speed of this transformation, approaches to the history of written constitutions have often been selective. Although they spread rapidly across maritime and land frontiers, constitutions are still usually examined in the context of individual countries. Although they could function as tools of empire, constitutions have generally been interpreted only in terms of the making of nations and nationalism. And although these are authored texts, written constitutions rarely attract the attention of literary scholars. Instead, these documents have become largely the province of legal experts and students of constitutional history, itself an increasingly unfashionable discipline. In this lecture, I examine the vital and various links between constitutions and print culture as a means of resurrecting and exploring some of the transnational and transcontinental exchanges and discourses involved in the early spread of these instruments. I also touch on the challenges posed to written constitutions – now embedded in all but three of the world's countries – by the coming of a digital age.[1]

Let me start with a seemingly familiar episode. Finally reaching a quorum on 25 May 1787, the fifty-odd delegates of the Philadelphia constitutional convention deliberately embraced seclusion. Armed guards surrounded their place of meeting, the red brick state house on the city's Chestnut Street. Although that summer was typically humid, and most of the delegates wore close-fitting uniform or formal dress, the windows of the state house were kept shut and covered over on the inside with heavy curtains. As for the green painted meeting room

---

[1] For more extensive discussion and documentation of some of the points raised in this lecture, see my *The Gun, the Ship, and the Pen: Warfare, Constitutions, and the Making of the Modern World* (2021). I thank Eric Foner, Hendrik Hartog, Jeremy Adelman, Daniel Hulsebosch, Dan Rodgers, Kim Lane Scheppele and Sean Wilentz for their expert advice and suggestions, and members of the Shelby Cullom Davis Center for Historical Studies at Princeton University and Perry Gauci's eighteenth-century seminar at the University of Oxford for comments on earlier versions of this paper.

itself, no spectators were admitted, and no journalists were allowed in systematically to report on the debates. The delegates themselves were under instructions not to pass on information to outsiders: 'Nothing spoken in the house' was to 'be printed, or otherwise published or communicated without leave'.[2] Not until 17 September was a complete draft of a *c.* 4,500-word constitution for the United States formally set down in red and black ink on four sheets of parchment, each about two feet wide and two feet high.

That same day, however, something of arguably greater global import occurred. A copy of this draft constitution was passed on to John Dunlap and David Claypoole, Revolutionary war veterans and proprietors of the first successful American daily, the *Pennsylvania Packet.* Two days later, on 19 September, Dunlap and Claypoole published the text of the draft constitution in full on this paper's front page. By late October, it had featured in over seventy other American newspapers; and, by the end of 1787, there had been at least 200 different printings.[3] Extracts were also increasingly filtering into print in other countries and continents. In this lecture, I want to investigate some of the consequences and meanings of these and later explosions of constitutional print, focusing on the years before the 1830s, but touching as well on subsequent developments.

## I

Written and engraved outlines of rules of government and codes of law and philosophies about them were ancient growths in many cultures. But the notion that 'a written constitution' should, in the words of a Victorian journalist, 'be broad, explicit, complete in itself', a discrete document possessing special status, that was widely circulated and that outlined the workings of a polity and certain rights, was a much later development.[4] Only from the mid-eighteenth century did political texts of this type begin proliferating at a more persistent rate. The United States constitution was not the first marker of this change. Gustaf III of Sweden, for example, issued his Form of Government in 1772. Widely publicised, and deliberately made available courtesy of the King's Printer in several languages, this explicitly endorsed the idea of a constitution as a supreme fundamental law to which the monarch himself was required to swear allegiance.[5]

[2] *Notes of Debates in the Federal Convention of 1787, Reported by James Madison,* with an introduction by Adrienne Koch (New York, 1987). The prohibition on disclosing information was made on 29 May.

[3] Pauline Maier, *Ratification: The People Debate the Constitution, 1787–1788* (New York, 2010), 70.

[4] *Gloucestershire Chronicle,* 2 December 1848.

[5] The official English translation was *Form of Government enacted by His Majesty the King and the States of Sweden Aug. the 21 1772* (Stockholm, 1772).

Nonetheless, the impact of the text crafted at Philadelphia over the summer of 1787 was unprecedented: and this was not simply because of its content, or because it had emerged out of a major revolutionary struggle turned global war.

It is suggestive that the new United States resembled Sweden in possessing both exceptionally high levels of literacy (at least among its white population) and a rapidly expanding print sector. American newspapers alone had doubled in number between 1760 and 1775, and would double again by 1790.[6] In addition, though, and unlike Sweden, the United States was a novel republic, confronted at once by acute domestic divisions and serious potential threats from without. It is this mix of circumstances – the scale both of American print culture and literacy levels and its post-independence internal and external fractures and challenges – that accounts for the extent to which print became a vital and calculated resource in the wake of the Philadelphia convention.[7]

The last article of its draft constitution stipulated that, in order to be ratified, it needed the approval of at least nine of the thirteen American states, all of them staging ratification conventions for this purpose. As is now well documented, securing this level of ratification for a controversial text put together in a secretive manner by representatives of still quasi-autonomous states proved a close-run thing. Final ratification was not achieved until September 1788.[8] The protracted uncertainty over the result meant that, for months on end, American activists and advocates invested substantial amounts of energy, cash, thought and printed words in publicising the content of the draft constitution and in publishing essays and polemics in its support. These domestic efforts were combined moreover with print campaigns outside the United States.

During the Revolutionary war, the American Congress and individual activists, notably Benjamin Franklin, had provided for the mass-printing and translation of the new republic's more emotive and innovative political documents and their busy distribution in Europe and elsewhere. As Daniel Hulsebosch and others have demonstrated, these overseas as well as domestic print campaigns were designed to convince foreign

[6] See Michael Warner, *The Letters of the Republic: Publication and the Public Sphere in the Eighteenth Century* (Cambridge, MA, 1990); and *The Colonial Book in the Atlantic World*, ed. Hugh Amory and David D. Hall (Cambridge, 2000), 361. For the wide levels of access to print in Sweden, see Marie-Christine Skuncke, 'Press Freedom in the Riksdag', in *Press Freedom 250 Years: Freedom of the Press and Public Access to Official Documents in Sweden and Finland – A Living Heritage*, ed. Bertil Wennberg *et al.* (Stockholm, 2018).

[7] For a recent survey of some of these pressures, see Max M. Edling, 'A More Perfect Union: The Framing and Ratification of the Constitution', in *The Oxford Handbook of the American Revolution*, ed. Jane Kamensky and Edward G. Gray (New York, 2013).

[8] See Maier, *Ratification*, *passim*.

governments and public figures of the significance of the new United States, the enlightenment of its political experiments, its determination to resist the British, and consequently its claims to be taken seriously as regards possible war loans, trade and military aid. From 1787, similarly ambitious and concerted campaigns were launched to publicise the new United States constitution.[9] American diplomats, consuls and merchant patriots systematically distributed copies of the text to foreign rulers and other major players; while duplicates of the constitution were regularly enfolded into American diplomatic correspondence. Writing to inform the powerful sultan of Morocco, Sidi Muhammad, of the final ratification of the new constitution in late 1788, George Washington was careful to add: 'of which I have the honour of herewith enclosing a copy'.[10] The official thinking behind such efforts was that powerful actors in foreign spaces would be at once impressed by the provisions of the constitution, and persuaded by them that the United States was now constructing a more effectual central government. This, it was hoped, would help to deter any potential armed invasions from without, while also working to reassure and entice overseas merchants and foreign investors in the new republic.

These more official and planned distributions of the American constitution overseas were swamped in volume however by coverage in foreign-based commercial print media. In this regard, the United States was able to benefit from the very empire it had violently rejected. There were naturally old and close links between American printers and publishers and their counterparts in Ireland and Britain. Because of this, and because of the commonalities in language, printed material issued in the United States regularly crossed the Atlantic. The text of its draft constitution featured in some London newspapers barely five weeks after its first appearance in the *Pennsylvania Packet*.[11] Since London was the world's biggest port, with the largest mercantile marine, newsworthy incoming American printed material was frequently shipped onwards, to other parts of Europe, Asia, West Africa, South America, the Caribbean, and ultimately to sectors of the Pacific world. Other European carriers,

---

[9] Daniel J. Hulsebosch, 'The Revolutionary Portfolio: Constitution Making and the Wider World in the American Revolution', *Suffolk University Law Review*, 47 (2014), 759–822; and see Daniel J. Hulsebosch and David M. Golove, 'A Civilized Nation: The Early American Constitution, the Law of Nations, and the Pursuit of International Recognition', *New York University Law Review*, 85 (2010), 932–1066.

[10] This letter by Washington crossed continents a further time, being printed in the *Calcutta Journal* in May 1822.

[11] Leon Fraser, *English Opinion of the American Constitution and Government, 1783–1798* (New York, 1915). The speed of the draft constitution's publication in London was made possible by one of the Philadelphia delegates carefully despatching his own early print copy there.

notably those of France, also helped to disseminate copies of the American constitution and commentary on it. But what about those on the receiving end? What were the long-term effects of so much published material on American constitutionalism relentlessly crossing maritime and land boundaries?

## II

There is no doubt that in the wake of the American Revolutionary War – which had itself commanded wide international attention and generated extensive reportage – the print coverage devoted to the work of the Philadelphia convention of 1787 helped both to publicise the concept of a single document constitution, and to advertise the advantages of providing for a close and ambitious relationship between a political text of this sort and print. One sign of this is the reaction of some political critics. From the 1780s, and still more after 1789 and the issue of successive written French constitutions, conservatives in Britain and some of the German lands increasingly began to refer dismissively to '*paper* constitutions': paper being, of course, at once the essential fuel of a printing press, and, in this partisan polemic, essentially frail and unreliable.[12]

There is no doubt, too, that over the long nineteenth century, the United States constitution proved a far more widely reproduced and translated text across continents than the American Declaration of Independence. In part this was because, outside of the Americas, declarations of independence remained sparse phenomena until after the First World War. Between 1790 and 1914, only ten countries outside the Americas appear to have chosen and been in a position to issue a document of this sort.[13] Written constitutions, by contrast, spread throughout this same period at an exponential rate, multiplying even faster in the wake of the First World War.[14] Because of its celebrity and content – and crucially too because of its capacity to endure – the American constitution was regularly reprinted in multiple languages precisely in part so as to serve as an aid to constitution-writers elsewhere. Thus, between April and September of the revolutionary year of 1848, while a new constitution for France was in process of manufacture, at

---

[12] See, for instance, the accusation by the anti-Jacobin John Bowles that the 'French ... paper constitution fell to pieces before they could well get it into their hearts', in his *Dialogues on the Rights of Britons* (London, 1793), 11.

[13] David Armitage, *The Declaration of Independence: A Global History* (Cambridge, MA, 2007), 145–55.

[14] For a partial collection, see the remarkable compendium masterminded by Horst Dippel: *Constitutions of the World: 1850 to the Present*, available in microform in multiple languages.

least seven different French translations are known to have been issued of the United States constitution.[15]

At times, these high and wide publicity levels encouraged other states and regions engaged in constitution-making to include provisions in their texts that were similar to those contained in the American constitution.[16] More common, though, was emulation of some of the same print strategies that American constitutionalists had earlier deployed. One sees both of these trends at work in the short-lived constitution issued in 1811 in Venezuela, the first South American region to declare its independence from Spain.

At one level, Venezuelan activists conspicuously appropriated some of the language and provisions of the American constitution, though still selectively. After invoking God (unlike the United States constitution) their own 1811 text begins: 'We the people of the states of Venezuela'. It goes on to provide for the founding of a new federal republic, and for the creation of a house of representatives and senate in Venezuela after the United States pattern. But, as happened in many other polities both within and outside South America, Venezuelan revolutionaries also borrowed the American tactic of compiling portfolios of their con-stitutional documents, and disseminating these in print in the hope of influencing opinion overseas. Together with other new political texts, a copy of the Venezuelan constitution drafted in Caracas was promptly shipped to London. Here, a bound edition entitled *Interesting Official Documents Relating to the United Provinces of Venezuela ... Together with the Constitution Framed for the Administration of Their Government* was published by Longmans in 1812, with Spanish and English versions on offer on alternate pages, ready for distribution among sympathetic and influential Britons, and for shipping onwards to multiple locations overseas.[17]

Like American legislators after 1776, those compiling this Venezuelan portfolio understood that constitutional texts could function as more than instruments for domestic law and governance. Once put into print, and widely disseminated, they could be a means of communicating identity and ideas across borders: devices by which a polity might pro-claim, promote and define itself in foreign as well as domestic spaces.

---

[15] Elise Marienstras and Naomi Wulf, 'French Translations and Reception of the Declaration of Independence', *Journal of American History*, 85 (1999), 1318 n.

[16] Though the degree to which this happened was limited and varied across world regions. The determination of many states outside the Americas before 1914 to provide in their constitutions for a monarchy of some sort and still more for parliamentary systems – both institutions alien to the United States – should be noted.

[17] The full text of the constitution is provided in Spanish and English in *Interesting Official Documents Relating to the United Provinces of Venezuela ... Together with the Constitution Framed for the Administration of Their Government* (1812), 151–298. The Venezuelan-born intellectual Andrés Bello, at this stage an exile in north London, played a major role in engineering the appear-ance of this publication.

As the compilers of the *Interesting Official Documents* made clear in 1812, without the writing of their constitution and its print distribution and export, Venezuelans 'could not have solemnly declared [their] … intention to the world'.[18]

## III

For all this activism and print ingenuity, the first Venezuelan republic quickly failed. Its lavish printed and circulated portfolio endured, however, forming part of what by now – the early nineteenth century – was a rapidly expanding print archive of different countries' constitutional projects: and this is a critical point. Attention has traditionally focused on how and how far the United States constitution itself provoked political, ideological, legal and institutional emulation elsewhere. Yet quite as important were the ways in which the wide distribution in print of this American text helped to bring into being both *other*, potentially competing constitutional systems in different parts of the world and *rival* written and printed constitutional texts.

As more and more states adopted and published written constitutions, and as some of these texts (never all) passed into multiple translations and editions and crossed borders, men and women interested in this kind of political technology were presented with a widening choice. Not only could they study and plunder the United States' own much reproduced and translated constitutional texts. Progressively, they were in a position also to obtain information on constitutions generated by other polities and, if they wished, borrow selectively from these as well. Already, by the late eighteenth century, savvy publishers were capitalising on this trend. Instead of merely publishing the text of a single political constitution, they began issuing omnibus collections of constitutions produced by several different countries.[19] This way, curious readers and aspiring constitution-makers could compare and contrast rival print and paper models of organising a state and its laws. The long-term consequences of this were many and mixed. Let me touch on just three of them.

First, and this is just one reason why cultural and literary scholars should pay closer attention to constitutions, the growing print availability not only of individual texts of this sort, but also of compendia of different constitutions fostered a rise in what can be styled informal or amateur constitution-writing and speculation. It became more common for

---

[18] *Ibid.*, 307.

[19] A pioneering example is Jacques Vincent Delacroix's widely translated *Constitutions des principaux états de l'Europe et des États-Unis* (2 vols., Paris, 1791). Compilations of American state constitutions were published in London, Glasgow and Dublin in 1782–3, and in America itself still earlier.

private individuals, possessed of sufficient literacy, time and enthusiasm, to embark on and sometimes publish their own attempts at a written constitution for real (and sometimes imagined) locations, just as they might attempt writing a novel or a pamphlet or a piece of journalism. Hence the possibly apocryphal story that, even when very young, Charles Stewart Parnell had busied himself sketching out constitutions for a free Ireland, which became part of his legend.[20]

But while such informal constitution-writing crossed territorial, linguistic and class boundaries, in advance of 1914 it appears to have remained a highly gendered cultural and political practice. There were certainly stray female radicals, such as Olympe de Gouges, who penned declarations of rights; while there are many more examples of women in some regions of the world drafting constitutions for charitable and religious organisations. In 1825, the wealthy Jewish philanthropist Rebecca Gratz, an American friend of the Anglo-Irish novelist Maria Edgeworth, both wrote and had published *The Constitution of the Female Hebrew Benevolent Society of Philadelphia*. But, after 1770 and before the First World War, there seem to be few examples of women anywhere across the globe designing unofficial political constitutions, even in the privacy of their own homes.[21]

Second, the degree to which *multiple* constitutions were put into print circulation from the late eighteenth century onwards resulted in a changed and evolving politics of extraction, appropriation, comparison and selection. Those actively engaged in planning and drafting constitutions, but also individuals wanting to imagine new systems of power, government and rights, were more and more able to adopt a policy of pick and mix. They could study and select between an assortment of ideas, institutions, laws and language set out in an expanding print array of different countries' constitutions. They could then meld and combine these borrowings and inspirations with their own indigenous ideas and domestic legal and political practices and priorities.

One can see this kind of pick-and-mix strategy at work at an official level in the making in 1814 of Norway's constitution, next to that of the United States the oldest such document still operating today, albeit in a much-amended form. As a late nineteenth-century Swedish jurist, Nils Höjer, meticulously charted, there were borrowings in this original 1814 Norwegian text, 'and in some cases verbatim translations', from the French revolutionary constitutions of 1791, 1793 and 1795, the United States constitution, the Polish constitution of 1791, the Dutch, Swedish

---

[20] I owe this information to Professor Roy Foster.

[21] Though Pasquale Paoli's revolution in Corsica in 1755 and written constitution that year did prompt the English radical Catherine Macaulay to include 'a short sketch for a democratical government in a letter to Signor Paoli' in her first political publication in 1769.

and Cadiz constitutions of 1798, 1809 and 1812 respectively, and more.[22] This same Norwegian constitutional moment also illustrates how, as communication technologies and networks evolved, so, too, did the ways in which print was drawn on to promote and shape responses to political constitutions. Norway's rulers, under pressure from Swedish armed invasions, provided for the final printed version of this 1814 constitution to be made available in the country's expanding network of urban and village post offices, so that men and women coming in to post or pick up letters and parcels could purchase their own copy, or study one while they waited. It was also officially recommended that Norwegians paste pages from these printed copies onto the interior walls of their houses, thereby aiding insulation and, quite literally, helping to domesticate the terms of this new constitution.[23]

My third point is this: made up of words, written constitutions were perfectly positioned for infinite reproduction and for transmission across borders and languages by means of print. This is a prime reason why these political devices have persisted and become almost universal. But since these *were* so often widely distributed political texts, they were always subject to multiple readings and interpretations, even in their countries of origin. Once translated and issued abroad, constitutions might become still more volatile, lending themselves to multiple uses and understandings. Take the way in which the Plan de Iguala promulgated in February 1821 was subsequently retooled in different locations by those contending against modes of empire.

## IV

This text, the Plan de Iguala, was originally issued by the Mexican warlord Colonel Agustín de Iturbide as a blueprint for the government of a future independent, though possibly still royalist, Mexico. But its twelfth clause, especially, proved eminently exportable and malleable: 'All the inhabitants of New Spain, *without any distinction between Europeans, Africans, or Indians*, are citizens of this monarchy, and have access to all employment according to their merits and virtues.' Once translated and set in motion in print, this section of the Plan de Iguala was sometimes adopted and adapted by those pressing for wider political rights for all males, irrespective of religion, skin colour, wealth, ethnicity or colonial status.[24]

[22] Kåre Tønnesson, 'The Norwegian Constitution of 17 May 1814: International Influences and Models', *Parliaments, Estates and Representation*, 21 (2001), 175–86.

[23] For these and other publicising techniques, see *Writing Democracy: The Norwegian Constitution, 1814–2014*, ed. Karen Gammelgaard and Eirik Holmøyvik (New York, 2015).

[24] A full translation of the Plan de Iguala is available online on Rice University's digital scholarship archive. In its original form, and like the Cadiz constitution of 1812, this confined religious toleration to Catholics.

Thus, in the autumn of 1821, an English-language version was published in the *Connaught Journal*, a liberal Catholic newspaper, which
offered its own interpretation of the plan's lessons for an Ireland where
most Catholic males were still excluded from voting and all were prohibited by law from standing for election to the Westminster parliament.
'How profitable a moral might our own country derive from th[is]
example,' declared the paper's editor:

> Ireland would not now exhibit a scene of wretchedness and despair, of deadly feuds and
> nightly murders, if that conciliatory spirit which dictated the twelfth article of the
> Mexican constitution pervaded the councils of our statesmen and legislators.[25]

By 1822, this kind of gloss on the wider significance and utility of the Plan
de Iguala had reached Calcutta, already one of the world's prime centres
of print. Along with translations of other new South American constitutions, the draft constitution of an independent Peru, for instance, and
part of the founding constitution of Gran Colombia, extracts from the
Plan de Iguala were published in the *Calcutta Journal*, the Indian subcontinent's first daily newspaper.[26] Its radical owners, the Englishman James
Silk Buckingham and Rammohan Roy, a high-status Kulin Brahman
from Bengal, chose to highlight the self-same clause in the plan that
the *Connaught Journal* had earlier found so compelling:

> All the inhabitants of New Spain, without any distinction of Europeans, Africans, *or
> Indians*, are citizens of this monarchy, and eligible in every office, according to their
> merit and virtue. [*sic*]

The word 'Indians' obviously meant something very different in Calcutta
than it did in Mexico, and this was the essential point. For Roy and
Buckingham, the Mexican Plan de Iguala offered useful ammunition
for some of what they were campaigning for within the Indian subcontinent itself:[27] not a rapid end to rule by the British East India
Company, which at this stage seemed to most Asian and European oppo-
sitionists beyond possibility; but rather, reforms in the company's government, and an altered British empire in which, 'without any distinction of
Europeans ... or Indians', all male groupings might be treated 'according to their merit and virtue'.

[25] As reported in the *Calcutta Journal*, 9 May 1822.

[26] On Calcutta's print culture and its mixed policies: Miles Ogborn, *Indian Ink: Script and
Print in the Making of the English East India Company* (Chicago, 2007); and P. Thankappan Nair,
*A History of the Calcutta Press, the Beginnings* (Calcutta, 1987). For the *Calcutta Journal*'s commen-
tary on and selective reprintings of (mainly) South American constitutions, see its issues for 7
September 1821, 6 April, 9 May, 9 November 1822 and 14 February 1823.

[27] For excellent introductions to these men and their political ideas, see Kieran Hazzard,
'From Conquest to Consent: British Political Thought and India' (Ph.D. thesis, University
of London, 2017); and C. A. Bayly, 'Rammohan Roy and the Advent of Constitutional
Liberalism in India, 1800–1830', *Modern Intellectual History*, 4 (2007), 25–41.

## V

Already by this stage, the 1820s, indeed, some optimistic observers were envisaging a future in which, primed by print, written and reforming constitutions might soon become ubiquitous. 'We shall see the Asiatic states demanding the representative system in a few years,' wrote one British radical, 'aye, and the African too.'[28] But while print was formative for the advance, shaping and take-up of written constitutions, by itself – even apart from the wide variations in its availability across the globe – print was manifestly never enough. The fact that the current United Kingdom, long one of the world's most prolific centres of print, still remains without a codified constitution today is itself a *qualified* demonstration of this point.[29] So, too, is the fact that, while China was a pioneer in the invention of both print and paper, successive Qing emperors and their bureaucracies continued to display minimal interest in written constitutionalism until the very end of the nineteenth century. An American merchant based in Macao made precisely this point when writing for the *Canton Miscellany* in 1831. 'Constitution manufacturers' were hard at work in Spain and Portugal and even in 'minor states' such as Hanover and Saxony, he remarked in his article, accurately enough. The 'paper manufactories in China', this writer went on, were 'surely equal' to publishing outlets in these European locations. So why, he implied provocatively, given that the necessary raw materials and technologies existed there in abundance, were no comparable paper and printed constitutions emerging from within the Qing empire?[30]

Print, in other words, was persistently an important influence on the evolution, format and dissemination of written constitutions. But, by itself, print was not enough. The interests, ideas and imperatives of those in possession of prime political, ideological and military power were of more decisive importance. As events in the 1820s demonstrated, considerations of power could easily constrain print's ability to foster new constitutional initiatives within the United States itself.

By this stage, the thirteen American states which the delegates at Philadelphia had taken for granted in 1787 had expanded to twenty-four, while the registered American population had tripled. Left out of the official census listings however were Native Americans. Not generally liable for tax, these peoples were not included among the United States citizenry. Neither in the main were they slaves. So, what were they?

---

[28] Richard Carlisle writing in *The Republican* (1820), 229–30.

[29] Qualified, because the surge in the publication levels of British constitutional histories from the 1820s onwards can be interpreted in part as a response to the accelerating issue, printing and publicity of new political constitutions in the Americas and sectors of Continental Europe by this stage.

[30] *Canton Miscellany* (Guangzhou, 1831), 32–4.

In 1827, leading activists among the 15,000 or so Cherokees, based largely on 9.5 million acres of land in the emerging state of Georgia, along with some sympathetic Protestant missionaries active amongst them, decided that what these people were in fact was an independent nation, and consequently that they required a written constitution.[31]

By now, the Cherokees had acquired access to print. One of their number, Sequoyah (about whom too little remains known), had invented a writing system which allowed the Cherokee language to be read, taught in schools, set down on paper and put into typescript.[32] One result of these innovations, along with local missionary activity and sponsorship, was that, in 1827, some leading Cherokee were able to hold a convention, and adopt and print 'a Constitution for [their] future government'. Like so many other constitution-makers, these men cut and pasted, quite deliberately replicating parts of the United States constitution. 'We, the *representatives* of the people of the *Cherokee nation* in Convention established' is how their constitution begins. But these Cherokee activists also set down in close geographical detail the territorial 'boundaries of this nation', which were 'hereafter [to] remain unalterably the same':

> Beginning on the North Bank of Tennessee River at the upper part of the Chickasaw old fields: then following the main channel of said river, including all the islands therein, to the mouth of the Hiwassee river, then up the main channel of the said river including islands, to the first hill which closes in on said river, about two miles above Hiwassee old town …[33]

But neither this particular vision of the land, nor the Cherokee claim to be a 'free and distinct nation' with the right to govern itself, gained traction. Both the United States federal government in Washington and the all-white Georgia legislature rejected the legality of this constitution and the validity of Cherokee national aspirations. 'The propriety of effecting an entire abolition of the exercise of governmental powers, by the Cherokee Indians', the members of the Georgia senate were assured in October 1830:

> Your committee consider as settled. The State [Georgia], by an act of her legislature, has extended her law, both civil and criminal; over the territory and persons of said Nation indiscriminately, and thereby virtually abolished all government over such territory save her own.[34]

Later in this same decade, the 1830s, most Cherokee were driven out of Georgia, and forcibly relocated further west, some 4,000 of them dying

---

[31] See William G. McLoughlin, *Cherokee Renascence in the New Republic* (Princeton, 1986).

[32] On Sequoyah and his background, see *An Extensive Republic: Print, Culture, and Society in the New Nation, 1790–1840*, ed. Robert A. Gross and Mary Kelly (Chapel Hill, 2010), 499–513.

[33] *Constitution of the Cherokee Nation, Formed by a Convention of Delegates* (New Echota, 1827).

[34] As reported in the *Cherokee Phoenix* (the first Native American newspaper) on 20 November 1830.

in transit. This can seem a distinctively American frontier tragedy. But it was more than that.

At one level, this Cherokee episode underlines yet again how closely and repeatedly access to print could be linked to interest and active participation in constitution-making. At another level, this same episode confirms how, in regard to constitutions, the opportunities and ideas made available and nurtured by print might be suppressed and sidetracked by those possessed of different identities or ideas and superior levels of power. This same episode is also an example of how written constitutions were sometimes closely bound up with varieties of empire-making and empire legitimation – in this case the forging of white American overland empire – and not simply with the business of nation-making and rising nationalism.

Yet this Cherokee initiative in the 1820s also makes clear that, as with print in general, written and printed constitutions were sometimes volatile entities. The involvement of missionaries in this Cherokee episode further reinforces this point. Over the course of the long nineteenth century, the work of missionaries in creating new written languages and introducing printing presses in parts of the Americas, Greater Asia, Africa and the Pacific world would contribute to different indigenous groupings adapting and experimenting with this device – a written constitution – for their own particular ends and in accordance with their respective cultural norms.[35] At no time was print ever an equal opportunity facility. But, to paraphrase the great political scientist Benedict Anderson, in part because of print, written constitutions proved 'an invention on which it was impossible to secure a patent'. Like other works and concepts susceptible to print, constitutions of this sort progressively became 'available for pirating by widely different, and sometimes unexpected, hands'.[36]

## VI

This brings me to my conclusion. As a publicity image for this lecture, I selected a wonderful photograph by Kim Ludbrook of a demonstrator in the South African capital city of Pretoria. The individual concerned, who was protesting in April 2017 against the then government of Jacob Zuma, was a member of the Economic Freedom Fighters (the EFF), a far left, pan-Africanist, sometimes violent grouping. Consequently, he was careful to conceal his personal identity from the photographer,

[35] For Pacific-world examples of missionary importation of printing presses from the 1810s being succeeded by indigenous rulers' experimentation with varieties of charters and constitutions, see my *The Gun, the Ship, and the Pen*, 284–305.

[36] *Imagined Communities: Reflecting on the Origin and Spread of Nationalism* (2006 edn), 67.

while simultaneously affirming his political allegiance. He hid his face behind a copy of a mass-produced version of the South African constitution, the text promulgated in 1996 by President Nelson Mandela which signalled the formal end of apartheid. The particular edition featured in this photograph has a rousing cover illustration of a renewed and diverse South African population emerging triumphantly and together out of the pages of a book – namely, the constitution. Smaller than your average paperback, this edition was also deliberately designed to be easily portable and cheap enough for general consumption.

Here, then, is an illustration of the continuing value of print in some contexts for the advance and implementation of constitutionalism. Yet, of course, growing numbers of us now inhabit societies where men and women get the bulk of their political information from a screen, not from the printed page. Moreover, the coming of a digital age is relentlessly bringing about a balkanisation of data and debate, with regard to politics and allegiance as much else. We are increasingly leaving behind the narrow-aperture world where individuals relied heavily for their political orientation on just a few television and radio channels, and on a few major 'national' newspapers and magazines. Instead, in many locations, there is now a cacophony of potential political influences and nostrums transmitted by way of multiple media and multiple voices. The implications of these ongoing changes for the status, operation and futures of political constitutions that have relied so heavily in the past on print networks require more analysis and attention.

These ongoing technological shifts also underline what has been a central theme of my paper: namely, that written constitutions have never only been devices to do with the business of law and government, important though these are. Written constitutions have also always been bound up with changing patterns of thought and cultural practices, with the histories of war, gender, race, social class, religion, literacy and literature, communications, empire and nation-making and more, as well as with shifting patterns of influence between different regions of the world. Existing abundantly now across the globe, both in draft and informal versions and in finished and implemented form, written constitutions are phenomena and sources that cry out for more searching, more imaginative and more cross-disciplinary and cross-frontier mining and exploration.

*Transactions of the RHS* 31 (2021), pp. 89–114 © The Author(s), 2021. Published by Cambridge University Press on behalf of the Royal Historical Society. This is an Open Access article, distributed under the terms of the Creative Commons Attribution licence (https://creative-commons.org/licenses/by/4.0/), which permits unrestricted re-use, distribution, and reproduction in any medium, provided the original work is properly cited.
doi:10.1017/S0080440121000050

# AN OTTOMAN ARAB MAN OF LETTERS AND THE MEANINGS OF EMPIRE, *c.* 1860

### By Andrew Arsan

READ 7 FEBRUARY 2020*

ABSTRACT. This paper returns to one of the germinal texts of nineteenth-century Arab political thought, Butrus al-Bustani's *Nafir Suriyya* ('The Clarion of Syria'). A series of broadsides published between September 1860 and April 1861, these reflected on the confessional violence that had rent apart Mount Lebanon and Damascus in mid-1860. As scholars have suggested, Bustani – now regarded as one of the pre-eminent thinkers of the nineteenth-century Arab *nahda*, or 'awakening' – here offered a new vision of Syrian patriotism, which formed part of a longer reflection on political subjectivity, faith, and civilisation. But, this paper argues, these texts can also be read as reflections on the changing workings of empire: on the imperial ruler's duties and attributes and his subjects' obligations and rights; on the relationship between state and population and capital and province; on imperial administrative reform; and on the dangers foreign intervention posed to Ottoman sovereignty. Drawing on the languages of Ottoman reform and ethical statecraft, as well as on imperial comparisons, Bustani argued against the autonomy some counselled for Mount Lebanon and for wholesale integration with the Ottoman state. These texts offer grounds for methodological reflection and for writing Ottoman Arab thought into broader histories of imperial political thought.

## I Introduction

In late September 1860, the Ottoman port of Beirut was still a city reeling from war. In the last days of May, brutal fighting had broken out between the Christian and Druze inhabitants of Mount Lebanon, whose ranges overhung the Mediterranean littoral. The conflict lasted barely a month. By the end of June, Druze fighters had prevailed over their opponents, leaving Christian localities like Zahleh and Dayr

*I am grateful to Margot Finn and the RHS Councillors for their invitation to give this lecture, to Sue Carr, Katherine Foxhall and Frances Andrews for their kind assistance, and to Andrew Spicer for his patience and kindness. I would also like to thank the participants in the Cambridge Middle East reading group for their comments and suggestions. I am especially grateful to Paul Anderson for organising this event, to Camille Cole and Hannah El-Sisi for their close, thoughtful engagement, and to Camille, Hannah and Will Ryle-Hodges for reading suggestions.

al-Qamar in ruins. The fighting in Mount Lebanon was soon followed by violence in Damascus, where crowds attacked the city's Christian quarters for two weeks in July, provoking panic on the coast.[1] Now, as summer drew to an end, the traces of war were still everywhere about Beirut. Thousands of refugees remained in makeshift settlements on its outskirts. In the pine forest to the south of the city lay the headquarters of the French expeditionary force that had landed in August, charged with restoring order after the 'crime[s] against civilisation' of the summer.[2] In Beirut itself, the Ottoman state's special envoy to its Syrian provinces, Fuad Paşa, established an extraordinary court to try Druze accused of having orchestrated the violence against Christians. On 22 September, several leading Druze notables gave themselves up for trial after three months at large. Four days later, the members of the international commission tasked with restoring peace to Syria met for the first time.[3]

It was amidst this tumult that a broadside appeared in Beirut on 29 September, just three days later. Under the title *Nafir Suriyya*, or 'The Clarion of Syria', its author urged his fellow Syrians to remember that 'you drink the same water and smell the same breeze, and the language that you speak and the earth on which you dwell and your interests and habits are but the same'. If 'you are now still drunk with drinking the blood of your brothers in the homeland and heedless of the enormity of the disasters that have befallen you, there is no doubt you will soon awaken from this foolishness and take stock of the meaning of ... the general interest'. Its author's intent, then, was 'to guide you to knowledge of your interest and the welfare of your country and to move your hearts to express the principles of true faith (*diyana*) in which you are believers'.[4]

More broadsides were to follow in a similar exhortatory, predicatory style over the coming months. In all, eleven appeared between September 1860 and April 1861. These ranged in content from attempts to consider the war's causes and to tally up the material and moral losses – and gains – it had occasioned, to appeals to provide urgent relief to those who still remained homeless as autumn turned to winter, disquisitions on the meaning of war, civil war and civilisation, and programmatic statements on the future government of Mount

[1]  Leila Tarazi Fawaz, *An Occasion for War: Civil Conflict in Mount Lebanon and Damascus in 1860* (Berkeley, 1993), 193. This remains the best account of the war of 1860, alongside Ussama Makdisi, *The Culture of Sectarianism: Community, History, and Violence in Nineteenth-Century Ottoman Lebanon* (Berkeley, 2000).
[2]  Anon., *La Question d'Orient. Un Homme et une solution* (Paris, 1860), 5. On this intervention, see Fawaz, *Occasion for War*, 164–92; Davide Rodogno, *Against Massacre: Humanitarian Interventions in the Ottoman Empire, 1815–1914* (Princeton, 2011), 91–117.
[3]  Fawaz, *Occasion for War*, 181ff., 196.
[4]  Al-Mu'allim Butrus al-Bustani, *Nafir Suriyya*, ed. Yusif Quzma al-Khuri (Beirut, 1990), 10–11.

Lebanon. But they returned insistently to their central themes, harping on the need to reform Syria's society and administration and to expunge prejudice from its inhabitants' spirits, replacing it with the genuine faith from which patriotism and concord could spring. All bearing the pseudonym *muhibb li-l-watan* – the 'lover of the homeland' – these were the work of the man of letters Butrus al-Bustani (*c.* 1818–1883).[5]

It is no exaggeration to say that Bustani occupies a pre-eminent – not to say canonical – position in the overlapping fields of Arab intellectual and literary history and the history of Arab political thought.[6] Born into a Maronite Christian family in the southern reaches of Mount Lebanon, he was educated at the Maronite seminary of 'Ayn Waraqa. In the 1840s he fell in with the American missionaries who had recently established a station in Syria and converted to Protestantism, his break with the Maronite Church consecrated by the martyrdom of his fellow convert As'ad Shidyaq. As Ussama Makdisi has shown, however, this traumatic event only reinforced Bustani's belief in freedom of conscience and his 'ecumenical' sense that a diverse range of religions were all 'equidistant

[5] For an English translation, see the excellent Butrus al-Bustani, *The Clarion of Syria: A Patriot's Call against the Civil War of 1860*, transl. Jens Hanssen and Hicham Safieddine (Berkeley, 2019). I rely here on Yusif Quzma al-Khuri's 1990 Arabic edition, Bustani, *Nafir Suriyya*. On the importance of treating these texts as broadsides, see Hala Auji, 'The Implications of Media: A Material Reading of Nineteenth-Century Arabic Broadsides', *Visible Language*, 53 (2019), 20–49.

[6] The literature is vast, but see in particular George Antonius, *The Arabic Awakening: The Story of the Arab National Movement* (1938), 63–8; Albert Hourani, *Arabic Thought in the Liberal Age* (Cambridge, 1962); Abdul-Latif Tibawi, 'The American Missionaries in Beirut and Butrus al-Bustani', *St Antony's Papers*, 16 (1963), 137–82; Leon Zolondek, 'Socio-political views of Salim al-Bustani (1848–1884)', *Middle Eastern Studies*, 2 (1966), 144–56; Butrus Abu Manneh, 'The Christians between Ottomanism and Syrian Nationalism: The Ideas of Butrus al-Bustani', *International Journal of Middle East Studies*, 11 (1980), 287–304; Jan [Jean] Dayah, *Al-Mu'allim Butrus al-Bustani: Dirasa wa Watha'iq* (Beirut, 1981); Stephen Sheehi, 'Unpacking Modern Arab Subjectivity: Reading al-Mu'allim Butrus al-Bustani's Nafir Suriya', *Arab Studies Journal*, 6 (1998), 87–99; Sheehi, 'Inscribing the Arab Self: Butrus al-Bustani and Paradigms of Subjective Reform', *British Journal of Middle Eastern Studies*, 27 (2000), 7–24; Rana Issa, 'Biblical Reflections in the Arabic Lexicon: A Very Modern Translation Phenomenon', *Babylon Nordisk Tidsskrift for Midtøstenstudier* (2012), 56–63; Nadia Bou Ali, 'Butrus al-Bustani and the Shipwreck of the Nation', *Middle Eastern Literatures*, 16 (2013), 266–81; Maya Issam Kesrouany, 'Stranded in Arabic: Robinson Crusoe in Beirut', *Comparative Literature Studies*, 52 (2015), 289–317; Jeffrey Sacks, *Iterations of Loss: Mutilation and Aesthetic Form, al-Shidyaq to Darwish* (New York, 2015), 78–90; Rana Issa, 'The Arabic Language and Syro-Lebanese National Identity: Searching in Butrus al-Bustani's *Muhit al-Muhit*', *Journal of Semitic Studies*, 62 (2017), 465–84; Nadia Bou Ali, 'Blesseth Him That Gives and Not Him That Takes: Butrus al-Bustani and the Mercy of Debt', *Modern Intellectual History*, 16 (2019), 443–69; the critical essays by Jens Hanssen and Hicham Safieddine in Bustani, *The Clarion of Syria*, trans. Hanssen and Safieddine; Peter Hill, *Utopia and Civilisation in the Arab Nahda* (Cambridge, 2020); and Ussama Makdisi, *Age of Coexistence: The Ecumenical Frame and the Making of the Modern Arab World* (Oakland, 2021), 64–74.

from a universal god', and he eventually broke with the 'Bible-men', as the missionaries were known locally.[7] Over the course of a long and busy life, Bustani was variously a translator, lexicographer, encyclopedist, orator, publisher and educator. He founded and ran learned societies, schools, printing presses and newspapers, and among his many published works were a new translation of the Bible, prepared with the American missionary Cornelius Van Dyck, primers in Arabic grammar and arithmetic, an edition of the Abbasid poet al-Mutannabi, a dictionary, a vast, multi-volume encyclopedia, and Arabic renditions of *Robinson Crusoe* and *Pilgrim's Progress*.[8]

In light of such commitments, scholars have tended to treat Bustani as the archetypal Arab reformer, whose work strove to explore the central questions of the *nahda*, or cultural 'awakening' of the late nineteenth and early twentieth centuries: how to refurbish the Arabic language to make full use of its vast lexical possibilities? How to renovate Arab culture under the emergent conditions of capitalist modernity and craft a new Arab subject capable of progress and civilisation? How to engage with the West without losing oneself? And how to give coherent shape to an Arab or Syrian nation?[9] Indeed, Bustani has often been regarded as a proto-nationalist, whose writings laid the foundations on which later, fuller constructions of Syrian and Arab identity were built.[10]

---

[7] Makdisi, *Age of Coexistence*, 66. See Tibawi, 'The American Missionaries in Beirut'; Ussama Makdisi, *Artillery of Heaven: American Missionaries and the Failed Conversion of the Middle East* (Ithaca, 2008); Christine B. Lindner, 'Negotiating the Field: American Protestant Missionaries in Ottoman Syria, 1823 to 1860' (Ph.D. thesis, University of Edinburgh, 2009).

[8] On Bustani's associational life, see Hill, *Utopia and Civilisation*, 30–36, 42–7; Butrus al-Bustani, *Al-Jam'iyya al-Suriyya li-l-'Ulum wa al-Funun* (Beirut, 1990); and Yusif Quzma Khuri (ed.), *A'mal al-Jam'iyya al-Suriyya 1868–1869* (Beirut, 1990). I am grateful to Peter Hill for providing me with a copy of the latter. On his educational work, see Jens Hanssen, 'The Birth of an Education Quarter: Zokak El-Blat as a Cradle of Cultural Revival in the Arabic World', in *History, Space and Social Conflict in Beirut: The Quarter of Zokak El-Blat*, ed. H. Gebhardt (Beirut, 2005), 143–74; and Hanssen, *Fin de Siècle Beirut: The Making of an Ottoman Provincial Capital* (Oxford, 2005), 164–71. On his publishing and journalism, see Ami Ayalon, *The Arabic Print Revolution: Cultural Production and Mass Readership* (Cambridge, 2016), 36–8; and Elizabeth Holt, *Fictitious Capital: Silk, Cotton, and the Rise of the Arabic Novel* (New York, 2017), 18–19.

[9] For critical reflections on this scholarship, see Jens Hanssen and Max Weiss, 'Introduction. Language, Mind, Freedom, and Time: The Modern Arab Intellectual Tradition in Four Words', in *Arabic Thought beyond the Liberal Age: Towards an Intellectual History of the Nahda*, ed. Jens Hanssen and Max Weiss (Cambridge, 2016), 1–38; Hill, *Utopia and Civilisation*, 1–17; Stephen Sheehi, 'Towards a Critical Theory of al-Nahdah: Epistemology, Ideology and Capital', *Journal of Arabic Literature*, 43 (2012), 269–98; Shaden Tageldin, 'Proxidistant Reading: Toward a Critical Pedagogy of the Nahḍah in US Comparative Literary Studies', *Journal of Arabic Literature*, 43 (2012), 227–68.

[10] For treatments of Bustani that frame his work in such terms, see Hourani, *Arabic Thought*, 99–101; Stephen Sheehi, *Foundations of Modern Arab Identity* (Gainesville, 2004),

This view is, to a significant extent, founded on readings of *Nafīr Suriyya*. These broadsides bore the deep imprint of the violence and dislocation Bustani had lived through. But they also form part of a longer reflection on citizenship, faith and community, on sin, duty and judgement, and on language, culture, civilisation and ethics, which left its inflection on earlier writings such as his translations of *Pilgrim's Progress* and the Bible, or his 'lecture on the morals and mores of the Arabs'.[11] It is perhaps unsurprising, therefore, that they have lent themselves to the view that they were, at heart, meditations on the meaning of *patria* – and, in particular, articulations of a Syrian patriotism which Bustani hoped could supplant the fanaticism that had rent asunder local society.[12] In part for this reason, they have acquired canonical status in Arabic political thought. Generations of readers have come back to them, seeking in their words the means to build a future after war and to construct a secular politics founded on fraternity among fellow citizens.[13]

I want to return here to the *Nafīr* to complicate these readings. As much as evidence of Syrian patriotism, I contend, these texts show Bustani as an imperial political thinker.[14] By this, I mean not just that, as scholars have long since shown, his primary loyalty lay to the end with the Ottoman Empire, nor that his sense of Syrianness did not conflict with this broader commitment but was fortified by it.[15] After

46–57; Nadia Bou Ali, 'Corrupting Politics', in *Islam after Liberalism*, ed. Faisal Devji and Zaheer Kazmi (2017), 47–8.

[11] For an English translation, see Stephen Sheehi, 'The Culture of the Arabs Today', in *The Arab Renaissance: A Bilingual Anthology of the Nahda*, ed. Tarek el-Ariss (New York, 2018), 5–13.

[12] Abu-Manneh, 'The Christians', 294. On the couplet of *watan* and *gharad*, see Jens Hanssen, '*Wataniyya* as an Antidote to Sectarianism', in Bustani, *The Clarion of Syria*, 53–62, esp. 60.

[13] See for instance Yusif Quzma al-Khuri, 'Kalimat ila al-Qari', in Bustani, *Nafīr Suriyya*, 5–7. For more on this, see Jens Hanssen, '*Nafīr Suriyya* in Arabic Historiography', in Bustani, *Clarion of Syria*, 35–44.

[14] On imperial political thought, see David Armitage, *Foundations of Modern International Thought* (Cambridge, 2013); Duncan Bell, *The Idea of Greater Britain: Empire and the Future of World Order, 1860–1900* (Princeton, 2007); Duncan Bell (ed.), *Victorian Visions of Global Order: Empire and International Relations in Nineteenth-Century Political Thought* (Cambridge, 2007); Richard Bourke, *Empire and Revolution: The Political Life of Edmund Burke* (Princeton, 2015); Uday Singh Mehta, *Liberalism and Empire: A Study in Nineteenth-Century British Liberal Thought* (Chicago, 1999); Sankar Muthu, *Enlightenment against Empire* (Princeton, 2003); Jennifer Pitts, *A Turn to Empire: The Rise of Liberal Imperialism in Britain and France* (Princeton, 2005); Pitts, *Boundaries of the International: Law and Empire* (Cambridge, MA, 2018); Andrew Sartori, *Liberalism in Empire: An Alternative History* (Oakland, 2014). For an effort in this direction by a historian of the Middle East, see Thomas Philipp, 'From Rule of Law to Constitutionalism: The Ottoman Context of Arab Political Thought', in *Arabic Thought*, ed. Hanssen and Weiss, 142–66.

[15] Hourani, *Arabic Thought*, 101; Abu-Manneh, 'The Christians', 289–91; Jens Hanssen and Hicham Safieddine, 'Butrus al-Bustani: From Protestant Convert to Ottoman Patriot and Arab Reformer', in Bustani, *The Clarion of Syria*, 28–9; Hill, *Utopia and Civilisation*, 96.

all, as Ussama Makdisi has reminded us, the only surviving portrait of Bustani, painted a week before his death, shows him wearing the fez of the Ottoman reformer, a *majidiyya* imperial medal proudly pinned to his chest.[16] More than this, I argue that the *Nafir* evinced a deep concern with the central questions of imperial governance: what should be the relationship between the imperial capital and the provinces in a polity characterised by its territorial extent and demographic variety? On what basis could the imperial state build an effective and cohesive system of government? What path, in other words, should administrative reform follow? What rights should imperial subjects possess, and what were the duties incumbent upon them? And how could the Ottoman state thrive in a world of empires, at a time when other polities were increasingly encroaching upon its sovereignty? To answer these questions, Bustani resorted not just to the language of the Tanzimat itself, which he wove into his own political vision, but also, it would seem, to older conceptions of ethical governance which still inflected Ottoman languages of state into the nineteenth century.[17] Furthermore, I argue that Bustani's broadsides were also an attempt to puzzle through a more immediate, practical and local question: what future should the government of Mount Lebanon pursue after the disaster of 1860? Here too Bustani fell back upon empire, rejecting the autonomist visions of Maronite clergymen and French diplomats and military officers in favour of wholesale integration into a reformed Ottoman state. In short, Bustani was not simply concerned here with limning a new vision for the 'integration of Syrian society' within the 'framework' of Ottomanism, but also with establishing a new relationship between local society and imperial state.[18]

## II Bustani as a thinker of empire

Reading Bustani as a thinker concerned with the changing workings of empire allows us to see him as a figure who lived in his own times – times that were, as the phrase has it, deeply out of joint – rather than as a pioneer whose writings foreshadowed later ideas of the nation. To make sense of Bustani's writings, in other words, we must read them synchronically, and not teleologically as links in a chain of conceptual transmission broken by the tragedies of the Arab twentieth century or proleptically as 'earlier "anticipations" of later' ideologies and

[16] Makdisi, *Age of Coexistence*, 44.

[17] Marinos Sariyannis, *A History of Ottoman Political Thought up to the Early Nineteenth Century* (Leiden, 2019); Linda Darling, *A History of Social Justice and Political Power in the Middle East: The Circle of Justice from Mesopotamia to Globalization* (Abingdon, 2011).

[18] Abu-Manneh, 'The Christians', 288.

imaginings of the Arab nation.[19] The 'problem-space' in which these texts took form was one that was shaped by the existence of empire.[20]

It is not just that, as Ussama Makdisi has suggested, Bustani was in many ways the 'embodiment of the Tanzimat', a figure whose works echoed the 'civilising' impulse of Ottoman reform even as they offered a less hierarchical and more 'secular [and] liberal' vision of 'coexistence' than that which imperial reformers were willing to countenance, reversing the Tanzimat's 'negative imperative ... to *not discriminate* into a positive injunction to *respect* diversity' as the foundation of active 'citizenship'.[21] More than this, his thought during these fraught months was concerned as much with the state as with society, giving rise to a series of urgent reflections on the workings of government, the shortcomings and potentiality of imperial reform, and the respective duties and expectations of imperial state and subject. His writings took as their own, to a degree hitherto unappreciated by scholars, both the *dirigiste*, rationalising ethos of the Tanzimat – the 'reorganisation' of the state, as the Ottoman military and administrative reforms of the mid-nineteenth century are known – and the older languages of virtuous governance on which it drew.[22] As Hala Auji has recently suggested, this was reflected even in his broadsides' visual grammar, which shared 'numerous ... similarities' with the Arabic translation of the 1856 decree Bustani prepared at the American Missionary Press in Beirut. For Auji, it is no coincidence that Bustani referred to his text as a *layyiha* or 'bill', the same term that contemporaries used for the Ottoman decrees posted in public squares, for the original copies of the *Nafir* 'resemble' his setting of the 1856 edict 'more than they do any other extant print medium from this period'.[23]

At the same time, Bustani's answers to the fundamental questions thrown up by imperial governance were shaped by the intensely eventful and traumatic political and social context in which he wrote.[24] This, too, posed urgent questions. Scholars have largely focused on the broader

---

[19] Quentin Skinner, 'Meaning and Understanding in the History of Ideas', *History and Theory*, 8 (1969), 3–53, at 11.

[20] David Scott, *Conscripts of Modernity: The Tragedy of Colonial Enlightenment* (Durham, NC, 2004), 4.

[21] Makdisi, *Artillery of Heaven*, 187; Makdisi, *Age of Coexistence*, 67.

[22] For a recent synthetic account of this period, see Douglas A. Howard, *A History of the Ottoman Empire* (Cambridge, 2017), 227–77. For a restatement of an older view, see Carter V. Findley, 'The Tanzimat', in *The Cambridge History of Turkey*, vol. IV, *Turkey in the Modern World*, ed. Reşat Kasaba (Cambridge, 2009), 9–37.

[23] Auji, 'Implications of Media', 35, 39–42.

[24] R. G. Collingwood, *An Autobiography* (Oxford, 1970 [1939]), 29–43. Quentin Skinner, 'A Reply to My Critics', in *Meaning and Context: Quentin Skinner and His Critics*, ed. James Tully (Cambridge, 1988), 284. On Bustani's participation in relief efforts in 1860, see Hanssen, *Fin de Siècle Beirut*, 166.

consideration to which Bustani returned repeatedly: how to salve the wounds of civil war and construct a new compact for a Syrian society rent apart by fanaticism? But it is clear that Bustani was also concerned with the question of Lebanon's future government, and of how best to overcome the ruinous legacies of a system that had given rise to the bloodletting of 1860.

Until the 1830s, Bustani's home region had been subject to a complex system of layered governance, in which local-born potentates enjoyed considerable fiscal and military powers.[25] In the early nineteenth century, this system was dominated by one man, Bashir al-Shihab, who had concentrated political and economic power in his own hands, curbing the authority of Druze dynasties like the Junblat, while bolstering that of Christian families like the Khazin and encouraging the activities of Christian merchants in market towns like Dayr al-Qamar and Zahleh.[26] This was an order founded on the dominance of an elite structured around complex gradations of rank, status and faction – and not around religious difference.[27]

The Egyptian occupation of Syria from 1830 to 1840, and the establishment of direct Ottoman rule in 1840, precipitated the collapse of this 'old regime'.[28] From the 1840s onwards Ottoman officials and European diplomats created a new political system for the mountain, founded on the assumption that religion was fundamental to its inhabitants' sense of self and that the confessional community should therefore serve as the basic building block of public life. Far from reflecting ancient distinctions, this gave rise to a distinctly novel 'culture of sectarianism'. As newfangled ideas of popular sovereignty and religious difference bled into each other, the mountain's Christians increasingly came to think of political representation and rights in the terms of popular sovereignty.

[25] On early modern governance, see among others Abdul-Rahim Abu-Husayn, *Provincial Leaderships in Syria, 1575–1650* (Beirut, 1985); Abu-Husayn, *The View from Istanbul: Lebanon and the Druze Emirate in the Ottoman Chancery Documents, 1546–1711*; Stefan Winter, *The Shiites of Lebanon under Ottoman Rule, 1516–1788* (Cambridge, 2010); Heather Ferguson, *The Proper Order of Things: Language, Power, and Law in Ottoman Administrative Discourses* (Stanford, 2018), 196–232.

[26] See William Polk, *The Opening of South Lebanon, 1788–1840: A Study of the Impact of the West on the Middle East* (Cambridge, MA, 1963); Iliya Harik, *Politics and Change in a Traditional Society: Lebanon, 1711–1845* (Princeton, 1968); Richard van Leeuwen, *Notables and Clergy in Mount Lebanon: The Khazin Sheikhs and the Maronite Church, 1736–1840* (Leiden, 1994); Fruma Zachs, *The Making of Syrian Identity: Intellectuals and Merchants in Nineteenth-Century Beirut* (Leiden, 2005), 11–38.

[27] Makdisi, *Culture of Sectarianism*, 28–50.

[28] The phrase is Ussama Makdisi's: Makdisi, ibid., 51. On the Egyptian occupation of Syria, see Polk, *The Opening of South Lebanon*, 83–212; Khaled Fahmy, *All the Pasha's Men: Mehmed Ali, His Army and the Making of Modern Egypt* (Cambridge, 1997), 1–40; Caesar Farah, *The Politics of Intervention in Ottoman Lebanon, 1830–1861* (2000).

By the late 1850s, Maronite clerics and laymen argued that Christians' demographic dominance, as well as the Shihabs' supposed conversion to Christianity, gave them the right to govern.[29] Christian commoners like the muleteer Tanyus Shahin, who in 1858 led the people of Kisrwan in revolt against their Khazin landlords, combined this communitarianism with a growing sense that elite families, whether Christian or Druze, had usurped the people's right to govern themselves. Shahin thus demanded not just 'full equality and complete freedom' from the landlords' exactions, but also the 'liberation of Christians from their servitude'.[30] Such language only exacerbated existing tensions over land and labour in mixed regions like the Matn and the Shuf, feeding a cycle of mutual recrimination that culminated in the conflict of 1860.[31]

Bustani's texts were a reflection on this tortuous history and an attempt to envision another future. As such, they sought to provide an alternative not just to local visions of reform and restoration, but also to the recommendations of the international commission constituted to 'seek the origin and cause of these events … [and] suggest modifications to the current order of things … in the government of the Mountain'.[32] Here, I argue, empire provided the answer as much as the question. For Bustani's later broadsides can be read as a rebuke to those who proposed cleaving off the mountain from Ottoman sovereignty and keeping its government on a confessional basis. Where Maronite clergymen and European diplomats and military officers called for the creation of an autonomous, if not independent, political unit, governed on a religious basis, Bustani counselled the mountain's subjection to the writ of a reformed and reforming Ottoman state.

At the same time, we should be wary of too reductive and temporally narrow an understanding of context, which regards reflective writings entirely as epiphenomenal products of their political and economic circumstances.[33] For the *Nafir* can also be read, not just as reflections

[29] Carol Hakim, *The Origins of the Lebanese National Idea 1840–1920* (Berkeley, 2013), 13–65.

[30] Fawwaz Traboulsi, *A History of Modern Lebanon* (2012 [2007]), 31.

[31] Marwan Buheiry, 'The Peasant Revolt of 1858 in Mount Lebanon: Rising Expectations, Economic Malaise and the Incentive to Arm', in *Land Tenure and Social Transformation in the Middle East*, ed. Tarif Khalidi (Beirut, 1984), 291–301; Caesar Farah, *The Road to Intervention: Fiscal Politics in Ottoman Lebanon* (Oxford, 1992); Ussama Makdisi, 'Corrupting the Sublime Sultanate: The Revolt of Tanyus Shahin in Nineteenth-Century Ottoman Lebanon', *Comparative Studies in Society and History*, 42 (2000), 180–208.

[32] 'Protocole de la première séance de la commission de Syrie, tenue à Beïrout, le 5 octobre 1860 (19 rébiul-ewel 1277)', in I. de Testa, *Recueil des Traités de la Porte ottomane avec les puissances étrangères depuis le premier traité conclu en 1536, entre Suléyman I et François I, jusqu'à nos jours* (8 vols., Paris, 1864–94), VI, 106.

[33] Omnia El Shakry, 'Rethinking Arab Intellectual History: Epistemology, Historicism, Secularism', *Modern Intellectual History*, 18 (2021), 547–72. See also Peter E. Gordon,

on and of the moment, but as interventions in a 'historically extended ... argument', a discursive tradition full of 'alteration' and disagreement.[34] As I will argue, there are tantalising signs that Bustani drew upon older ideas of ethical and wise government, refurbishing them to make them fit for his own times. It is clear, then, that categorical distinctions between intellectual reflection and political engagement, which treat one or another of these as determinant, are of little help here.[35] For Bustani's writings of 1860 were at once commentaries on the pressing concerns of the present and attempts to construct a normative basis for political and ethical conduct. As such, they present an opportunity to rethink the workings of context and the relationship between praxis and norm-making, while integrating Ottoman Arab thought into broader histories of imperial political thought.[36]

## III Writing the Tanzimat: imperial patriotism and civic responsibility[37]

Much of the case for Bustani as a Syrian patriot rests on the *Nafir Suriyya*, which recent scholarship continues to treat as an attempt to imagine an 'Arab national subject' and a new 'positive definition of the nation' for 'Levantine society'.[38] Indeed, even those who acknowledge the imperial dimension continue to treat him as, ultimately, 'the first Syrian nation-alist'.[39] There is no disputing that these eleven broadsides were, at a fundamental level, concerned with elaborating a new kind of local community of feeling. After all, as their title suggests, it was for Syria that they sounded the alarm. Equally suggestive is the epithet Bustani gave his pieces: *wataniyyat*, or patriotic letters. Each opened in the same way,

'Contextualism and Criticism in the History of Ideas', in *Rethinking Modern European Intellectual History*, ed. Darrin McMahon and Samuel Moyn (Oxford, 2014), 35–55.

[34] David Scott, *Refashioning Futures: Criticism after Postcoloniality* (Princeton, 1999), 10.

[35] Andrew Arsan, 'Under the Influence? Translations and Transgressions in Late Ottoman Imperial Thought', *Modern Intellectual History*, 10 (2013), 375–97, at 384–5. See also Hussein Omar, 'Arabic Thought in the Liberal Cage', in *Islam after Liberalism*, ed. Faisal Devji and Zaheer Kazmi (2017), 17–18.

[36] For efforts in a similar direction by historians of international law, see Lâle Can and Michael Christopher Low, 'The "Subjects" of Ottoman International Law', *Journal of the Ottoman and Turkish Studies Association*, 3 (2016), 223–34; Aimee M. Genell, 'The Well-Defended Domains: Eurocentric International Law and the Making of the Ottoman Office of Legal Counsel', *Journal of the Ottoman and Turkish Studies Association* 3 (2016), 255–75; Umut Özsu, 'Ottoman International Law?', *Journal of the Ottoman and Turkish Studies Association*, 3 (2016), 369–76.

[37] I borrow here from Milen Petrov's notion of 'speaking Tanzimat'. Milen Petrov, 'Everyday Forms of Compliance: Subaltern Commentaries on Ottoman Reform, 1864–1868', *Comparative Studies in Society and History*, 46 (2004), 730–59.

[38] Sheehi, 'Unpacking Modern Arab Subjectivity', 88; Bou Ali, 'Butrus al-Bustani', 267.

[39] Abu-Manneh, 'The Christians', 294.

with a call to Bustani's 'fellow countrymen' – *abna' al-watan*, 'the sons of
the homeland' – a form of address that he used repeatedly to punctuate
each new section. And each had the same signature, *muhibb li-l-watan*,
'lover of the homeland', anonymity here a function of Bustani's desire
to stress patriotism as an article of faith.[40] What's more, Bustani made
explicit the scope of this 'homeland'. In September 1860, he declared
that 'Syria … with all its plains and desolate places, its coastlines and
mountains, is our homeland. And the inhabitants of Syria, of various
religious persuasions and origins and groupings are the sons of our
homeland.'[41] By his last broadside, Bustani had distilled this still-
complex vision of patriotic belonging into a purer formula, writing
simply of 'the people of Syria, our countrymen'.[42]

The evidence that these texts were, first and foremost, expressions of a
new understanding of Syrian patriotism appears overwhelming. I do not
want to suggest, therefore, that such readings are somehow wrong-
headed; on the contrary, they are entirely legitimate. But I do want to
add another layer of interpretation here, by arguing that, nested
within these dense, allusive, sometimes repetitive texts, there was also
another vision of belonging to the Ottoman Empire, or *mamlaka*. This
worked its way into Bustani's language and shaped his sense of the relationship between society, homeland and state as one that was fundamentally hierarchical and founded as much on duties as on rights.

Thus, Bustani redeployed the political language of Ottoman reform,
with its conception of the state as a benevolent protector, even when
he was considering the ties binding the territorial *patria* to its inhabitants.
In his fourth broadside, Bustani wrote that first among the 'obligations
the homeland owes its people' was 'security for their most important
rights, their [life and] blood, honour, and wealth (*damihim wa 'irdihim
wa malihim)'.[43] As Peter Hill has pointed out, these were the self-same
rights enshrined in the 1839 Gülhane edict, with its call for 'new laws'
that would ensure the 'security of life and soul and the preservation of
honour, conscience, and wealth' – *emniyet-i can ve mahfuziyyet-i ırz u
nâmûs u mal*.[44] The 1856 reform edict that so impressed Bustani
reaffirmed the imperial state's commitment to protect the 'life, wealth
… and honour' of 'all the subjects of our realm without exception'.[45]
Bustani's order of priorities here, then, is precisely that of imperial

[40] See for instance Bustani, *Nafir Suriyya*, 9–11.
[41] Ibid., 21.
[42] Ibid., 69.
[43] Ibid., 22.
[44] Hill, *Utopia and Civilisation*, 109. www.muharrembalci.com/hukukdunyasi/belgeler/
233.pdf (last accessed 10 April 2021).
[45] www.muharrembalci.com/hukukdunyasi/belgeler/231.pdf (last accessed 10 April
2021).

reform. Even when seemingly absent from Bustani's vision, the state remained a presence, haunting his prose and shaping his conception of what the people were owed.

What has not hitherto been appreciated, however, is that Bustani's subsequent invocation of 'civil, moral, and religious rights, not least the right to freedom of conscience in the matter of religious persuasion (*hurriyyat al-damir fi amr al-madhhab*)', was also an invocation of the 1856 decree, with its commitment to guaranteeing 'every denomination (*mezhab*)' 'perfect freedom' of belief.[46] This is not to claim that Bustani's stress on freedom of religion was not born of his own experience as a Protestant and his grief at the martyrdom of his fellow convert, As'ad Shidyaq.[47] Rather, it is simply to suggest that Bustani voiced this commitment in the language of imperial reform. Neither of these two contexts – the eventful, lived, intensely affective context of personal and local experience, and the linguistic, normative context of imperial decrees and administration – took precedence over the other in Bustani's writings. On the contrary, they were interwoven to create a powerful vision of the rights and duties of the individual subject.

Here, Bustani was not pushing the state to go further than it was prepared to go or sketching out a new horizontal conception of Syrian citizenship.[48] Rather, he was urging his fellow Syrians to regard the rights enshrined in the decrees of 1839 and, especially, 1856 as their own – to enjoy freedom of religion, but also to remember that these rights should not be abused or misconstrued, and that they entailed duties and constraints on individual subjects' comportment. Jens Hanssen is thus certainly correct to argue that Bustani was promoting here 'a contract of rights and duties between the inhabitants and their homeland'.[49] This is plainly apparent from Bustani's insistence that 'the people have binding rights and claims (*huquq*) on their *patria*, just as the *patria* [imposes] obligations on its people'. But if the people were to be given 'a hand in the affairs' of their country, it was precisely because this 'responsibility' would increase their 'concern for its progress'.[50] This, then, was a vision of 'active citizenry' that placed a great deal of weight on commitment to the commonweal.[51] 'Love of the homeland' should take precedence over 'religious fanaticism', and Syria's 'welfare'

[46] Bustani, *Nafir Suriyya*, 22; www.muharrembalci.com/hukukdunyasi/belgeler/231.pdf (last accessed 10 April 2021).

[47] Hill, *Utopia and Civilisation*, 109; Makdisi, *Artillery of Heaven*, 199–205.

[48] Ussama Makdisi, 'After 1860: Debating Religion, Reform and Nationalism in the Ottoman Empire', *International Journal of Middle East Studies*, 34 (2002), 601–17, at 606–8; Hill, *Utopia and Civilisation*, 101.

[49] Hanssen, '*Wataniyya* as Antidote to Sectarianism', 58.

[50] Bustani, *Nafir Suriyya*, 22.

[51] Hill, *Utopia and Civilisation*, 109.

over 'personal inclinations' – *ghayyat shakhsiyya*, Bustani using here, in his punning, allusive way, a term also connoting error and sin.[52] Bustani clearly did conceive of his Syrian compatriots as rights-bearing subjects. His understanding of these rights, however, was closely modelled on that of the reforming Ottoman state. What's more, he saw these rights as always entailing concomitant duties – to one's fellow countrymen, to the homeland and, as I will argue below, to the imperial state.

For while Bustani's fourth broadside focused on the relationship between the Syrian land and its people, at other moments he strove to consider their place within the overarching structures of imperial rule. This is true not just of rote invocations of imperial munificence like that which opened his second broadside in September 1860, with its praise for Sultan Abdülmecid's 'beneficent intentions' to ensure 'comfort, security, and justice' for all members of his 'flock' 'without exception'.[53] At a more fundamental level, Bustani's stress on the relationship between the territorial homeland and the imperial state shaped both his aetiological analysis of Syria's maladies and his prescriptions for a ravaged society. This is apparent from his fifth broadside, in which he considered at length the causes of the events of 1860. It was not just that Syria's inhabitants were 'a cluster of tribes of varying places, temperaments, prejudices, and interests, the majority of whom care not for the general interest'. To compound matters, the 'peripheries of the land were far from the centre of government, that is to say the capital of the empire (*mamlaka*)' and their 'governance was left to groupings (*aqwam*), many of whom, as history informs us ... did a great deal of harm to the lands under their rule, perpetrating acts of corruption and destruction'.[54]

The effects of this were plain to see 'when we open ... a book giving news of this land' – perhaps, as Peter Hill suggests, Tannus Shidyaq's chronicle *Akhbar al-A'yan fi Jabal Lubnan*, which Bustani had recently edited.[55] For Syria's history was 'full of wars and disasters', and 'blind' 'prejudice' stains every page 'like a black ugly spot'. 'This malicious principle', Bustani went on, 'takes on a different colour in each age.' In earlier times, it had attached itself to 'names like Qaysi and Yamani and then Junblati and Yazbaki' – for Shidyaq the main factions of elite politics in early modern Mount Lebanon.[56] 'More horrid' still was

---

[52] Bustani, *Nafir Suriyya*, 22.

[53] Ibid., 13.

[54] Ibid., 26.

[55] Hill, *Utopia and Civilisation*, 114. Tannus Shidyaq, *Kitab Akhbar al-A'yan fi Jabal Lubnan*, ed. Butrus al-Bustani (Beirut, 1859).

[56] Kamal Salibi, *A House of Many Mansions: The History of Lebanon Reconsidered* (1988), 115–17. Axel Havemann, *Geschichte und Geschichtsschreibung im Libanon des 19. und 20. Jahrhunderts: Formen und Funktionen des historischen Selbstverständnisses* (Beirut, 2002).

'the form' that prejudice had taken 'these past few years, when it had consumed once-sacred epithets like Nazarene [Christian] and Druze, and then Muslim and Christian'. For Bustani, local prejudices – whether of faction and family or religion – had for too long been the motive force of Syrian history. For all that there were many people of 'morals and quality' among its inhabitants, left to its own devices Syria could not but succumb to this 'evil'. Only one path could provide real 'hope of progress and civilisation' and allow the inherent 'qualities' of the majority to prosper: 'plac[ing]' the country under special measures, by imposing 'reforms (*tanzimat*) befitting the time and circumstances, and whose aim is the welfare of the land and the comfort of the subjects'.[57]

On the one hand, it is clear that the *Nafir* was an 'antisectarian' appeal to 'build a cohesive and "civilised" Syrian society'.[58] In such passages, Bustani developed a searing historical critique, both of the 'old order' that had prevailed until the early nineteenth century and the new 'culture of sectarianism' that emerged from the 1840s on. As dangerous as a system of government founded on inherited status and rank was one built on the confessionalisation of social life, the reduction of religious belief to sectarian prejudice, and the elevation of prelates to the position of temporal rulers. Both were equally ruinous, stymieing Syria's potential for civilisation. On the other hand, it is rather less certain that what he aimed for was a new 'social contract' in which Ottoman 'absolutist monarchy' would give way to the 'logic of the modern nation-state'.[59] For it is striking that Bustani did not see the imposition of direct Ottoman rule as in any way responsible for the events of 1860. On the contrary, he regarded this violence as, at least in part, born of Syria's political autonomy and remoteness from the centres of imperial sovereignty. Nothing could be done to overturn the tyranny of distance. But it could still be hoped that the *watan* – the homeland – could be integrated more fully within the *mamlaka* – the imperial realm – through a programme of thoroughgoing and just reform, which would expunge for once and for all the forces of prejudice from Syria.

### IV Against autonomy: Mount Lebanon in the *Nafir*

Indeed, this was not the only instance in which Bustani's language provides evidence of his endorsement of effective imperial reform as the only means of salving Syria's wounds and restoring order to Mount Lebanon.

[57] Bustani, *Nafir Suriyya*, 26–7.
[58] Jens Hanssen and Hicham Safieddine, 'Introduction: Translating Civil War', in Bustani, *Clarion of Syria*, 2.
[59] Bou Ali, 'Blesseth Him That Gives', 11, 24.

In November 1860, he reiterated his call for 'appropriate laws and just reforms, which suit the circumstances, the place and the time'.[60] At one level, this appears a straightforward use of the stock phrases of administrative parlance, with their rote invocation of the need to devise ordinances befitting the time and place.[61] At the same time, however, this can be read as a call to place Mount Lebanon in the grip of a strong, reforming central state. It is in this light that we can read Bustani's calls for 'appropriate laws (*shara'i mutfiqa*) and just reforms (*tanzimat 'adila*)'. The measures needed to address Mount Lebanon's predicament were not, for Bustani, the bespoke protocols devised by partisans of Mount Lebanon's administrative autonomy. Quite the opposite: the moment demanded that the state fulfil the commitments spelled out in grand edicts like those of 1839 and 1856 and continue with the thoroughgoing reorganisation, rationalisation and homogenisation of government. In other words, the reformed administration of Mount Lebanon and Syria should follow the imperial norm, rather than the devolved exception.

This is apparent from Bustani's insistence that the empire's laws and regulations should not be 'admixed with confessional laws' and that 'judgments [should] consider the particulars of the case and not the person'. Legislation should be 'rigorous, vigilant, and capable of keeping each [subject] within his limits'. But it should also 'look equally on every class of subject, granting no recognition to religious sects other than that accorded to their members' religious, moral, and civic rights, and the defence of these rights as such, and not by virtue of their connection to any person or group'.[62] Here, Bustani can again be seen restating the programme of the 1856 reform edict, with its commitment to erasing 'every distinction or designation tending to make any class whatever of the subjects of my Empire inferior to another class, on account of their religion', to ensuring freedom of religion, and to creating mixed courts for the judgement of 'all commercial, correctional, and criminal suits' involving members of different religious communities.[63]

This too can be read as an intervention in debates on the future status of Mount Lebanon. Against those who insisted that the region should retain its own administration founded on the principle of confessional distinction, Bustani argued that it should be folded fully into an empire-wide system of universal and impersonal procedural norms that would ensure equal judicial treatment for all. Religious difference should be respected as sacrosanct, but no single confessional group

---

[60] Bustani, *Nafir Suriyya*, 38.

[61] I am grateful to Camille Cole for pointing this out.

[62] Bustani, *Nafir Suriyya*, 38.

[63] www.anayasa.gen.tr/reform.htm (last accessed 10 April 2021).

should be accorded special status. To overcome the strife that had torn local society limb from limb and allow the wounds of sectarian hatred to close over, it was necessary to pursue the path of imperial reform to its fullest expression, rather than retreating into self-government founded on the weighted representation of different communities.

We do not need to look far for evidence that Bustani took seriously the potential of Ottoman bureaucracy. For his penultimate broadside treated the state as one of the primary agents of social transformation, setting out an expansive programme for a new regime of imperial sovereignty. He thus insisted on the 'need for governors to show circumspection and vigilance in the exercise of their mission, and to take steps to prevent events before they occur'. In an implicit criticism of the actions of Fuad Paşa, who had sentenced Druze notables to death on the basis of lists drawn up by Christian villagers, Bustani insisted it was not enough 'to execute the first killer … or to pin the responsibility on the administrator of the province or district where the violence occurred'.[64] Far more effective than this organised score-settling was a system of government that might prevent such 'strife' from occurring in the first place. For 'the country' could find 'repose and success' only in 'secure and favourable circumstances'. This was, once again, a deliberate echo of mid-nineteenth-century imperial decrees that harped on the need for 'security'. But it was also, in a way, a rebuke of the approach Ottoman administrators had taken in 1860. What was needed was the ideal vision of reformed government presented in official pronouncements, of 'governors who believe in the right of the state and the law of the country and the people, and who possess the ability, the will, and the means, both personal and military, to implement the laws and to punish offenders', rather than the 'reliance' shown on 'principles of division' drawn from the 'dark ages of despotism'.[65] To pit Christian against Druze by giving in to demands for 'retribution', let alone to make confessionalism the keystone of Mount Lebanon's government, would be a mistake.[66]

It followed from this that 'a barrier' should be erected separating 'spiritual power from statecraft or civil power'. Whereas spiritual 'leadership' (*al-ri'asa*) was 'by nature … invariable', 'governance [was] related to external and changing matters'. As only the latter was 'susceptible to alteration and reform', it alone was capable of bringing 'process and civilisation'. Inflexible and unresponsive to 'circumstances', religious leadership could lead only to stagnation. It was not that there was no place for religion in social life – quite the contrary. But combining spiritual and

---

[64] On Fuad Paşa's actions, see Fawaz, *Occasion for War*, 181ff.
[65] Bustani, *Nafir Suriyya*, 55–6.
[66] Ibid., 45.

religious authority would only attract unsuitable candidates, thus corrupting both true religion and statecraft, undermining faith in these
'most important and noble' of tasks and sowing 'discord'. Under 'spiritual leaders who could agree only to disagree', 'the people' were 'like a
flock without a shepherd', stripped all at once of legitimate government
and spiritual guidance.[67]

Bustani protested – too eagerly, perhaps – that he had no particular
community in mind, but spoke 'of all the many spiritual leaders of our
country, Muslim and Christian, Druze, Nusayri, Isma'ili, Yazidi,
Jewish, or Samaritan'.[68] It is hard, however, not to see this as an
attack on the Maronite Church's growing pretensions to political authority. Since the 1840s, churchmen had increasingly argued that Mount
Lebanon was, in history and population, a Christian land. It followed
from this, both that the Maronite Church was the natural representative
of the people and that the country should be governed by a Christian
ruler reflecting its culture and demographic make-up.[69] To the dismay
of men such as Tubiya 'Awn, the Maronite archbishop of Beirut, this
vision of Mount Lebanon as a Christian land had slipped out of their
grasp in 1860 when it was taken up by subaltern agents like the muleteer
Tanyus Shahin.[70] Now, amidst the ruins, figures like the Maronite patriarch, Bulus Mas'ad, and the archbishop of Saida, 'Abdallah al-Bustani,
attempted to reassert their control over their community, portraying
themselves to Ottoman authorities and French diplomats as the
Maronites' legitimate representatives.[71] In the *Nafir*, Bustani urged his
countrymen to renege on this vision and to follow the precedent of the
'civilised countries that have taken stock of the dangers of this admixture,
and who have created a separation between these two powers so that
neither counteracts the other's public benefits'.[72]

For Syria and Mount Lebanon to be governed effectively, sovereignty
over the people should not be divided among the religious leaders of each
community but concentrated in the hands of the imperial state. Indeed,
Bustani insisted that the sultan's 'righteous power' should reign supreme,
for neither 'true religion nor statecraft (*siyasa*) provided any grounds for
his subjects, whatever their background, to fail to give it due respect and
consideration'. There was no room in Bustani's vision for consultation or
representation. For as he explained, should imperial decrees 'be subject
to the will of the people and their diverse desires and varying prejudices'

[67] Ibid., 58.
[68] Ibid., 58.
[69] Hakim, *Origins*, 13–63.
[70] Makdisi, *Culture of Sectarianism*, 112–113.
[71] Hakim, *Origins*, 65–98.
[72] Bustani, *Nafir Suriyya*, 58.

they would quickly lose all persuasive force, holding 'great meaning' for some and none at all for others.[73] Bustani's vision of the new relationship between the locality and the imperial centre, then, was deeply hierarchical. Against the autonomy that some were advocating for Mount Lebanon and Syria, he insisted on subjection to the singular will of the sultan, the better to break the clergy's overweening influence over their flock.[74] Far from the liberal, egalitarian dispensation that some have discerned in Bustani's writings, this was a frank endorsement of the munificent authority of an autocratic state.[75]

If this separation between local clerical authority and imperial sovereignty was one element of Bustani's vision, another was his opposition to inherited status. He thus called for 'the granting of administrative positions on the basis of merit and aptitude, rather than nationality, descent, wealth or status'. To entrust administrative office to figures of 'lofty rank' on the basis of the 'majesty of the founder' of their 'tribe or dynasty' was a mistake, for these figures' belief that 'precedence' was theirs by right of birth and contempt for their perceived inferiors rendered them 'unsuitable' for office. As careful observation of the 'conditions of states' showed, government founded on inherited status led inexorably towards 'decline', while a system that accorded positions to 'those who deserve them, and not on the basis of inheritance' was assured of steady progress.[76]

It is again important to situate these arguments within a local context. Bustani was writing in February 1861, at a time when various schemes for the future of Mount Lebanon were being floated. One was that of the commander of the French expeditionary force to Syria, General Beaufort d'Hautpoul, who advocated the creation of a quasi-independent Lebanon under the aegis of Amir Majid Shihab, a scion of the family that had dominated the administration of Mount Lebanon until the 1840s.[77] To demonstrate the purported legitimacy of his plan, Beaufort circulated a petition through the mountain calling for the right of the Lebanese to be governed by a Christian prince and the restoration of the Shihabi dynasty.[78] Another was that of Patriarch Mas'ad, who shared Beaufort's vision of an autonomous Lebanon under a Christian governor, but favoured his own candidate, Yusuf Karam, himself the son of a family of standing from the mountain's northern reaches.[79]

[73] Ibid., 56.

[74] Hakim, *Origins*, 83–90.

[75] For an account that stresses liberalism in all its contradictions, see Bou Ali, 'Blesseth Him That Gives'.

[76] Bustani, *Nafir Suriyya*, 57.

[77] Hakim, *Origins*, 83–7.

[78] Ibid., 87.

[79] Ibid., 88–90.

Here, Bustani marked his opposition to these schemes of princely government. And he did so by resorting again to the language of the 1856 imperial rescript, with its declaration that 'all the subjects of my Empire, without distinction of nationality, shall be admissible to public employments, and qualified to fill them according to their capacity and merit'.[80] In weaving the rhetoric of imperial reform into his own prose, Bustani sought to ensure the creation of a new social order in Mount Lebanon and Syria by their wholesale integration into a reformed imperial polity.

## V Looking backwards: imperial ethics and just administration

In articulating this vision of the relations between centre and province and state and people, however, Bustani did not simply redeploy the language of the Tanzimat, but also an older way of thinking about governance. This is apparent from his eighth broadside. In this text, which appeared in November 1860, he wrote that among the many baleful consequences of the late 'civil war' was

> the loss of the mutual support (*arkan*) between ruler and ruled, and between subjects (*ri'aya*) and their government. For it is well known that the trust of those who govern the matters [of state] in the people depends in great part on the trust (*irkan*) of the people in them, and vice versa.

'Hope' for progress, then, resided 'on the one hand … in the wisdom of rulers, the excellence of their administration (*husn idaratihim*), [and] the reform of their conduct towards their subjects'. But while progress was contingent on rulers' capacity to 'show consideration' towards those they ruled, it also depended on 'the people's knowledge of their own welfare, [and] avoidance of … excess in asking for what is forbidden by ethical government, true religion, and morals (*siyasa wa diyana wa adaban*)'.[81]

At one level, this vision of restraint and mutual trust did track the reforming Ottoman state's own perception of itself. Thus, Bustani's language here followed that of the 1839 Gülhane edict, with its declaration that only 'new laws' would ensure 'excellence of administration (*hüsn-i idaresi*)', enabling the well-protected domains to regain their 'prosperity and strength'.[82] However, it is telling that this expression, which did not recur in the 1856 reform edict, was drawn from an older lexicon of

---

[80] www.anayasa.gen.tr/reform.htm (last accessed 10 April 2021).

[81] Bustani, *Nafir Suriyya*, 45.

[82] I use here Halil İnalcık's translation in *Sources in the History of the Modern Middle East*, ed. Akram Khater (Belmont, 2011), 12; and the Ottoman text in Latin characters available at www.muharrembalci.com/hukukdunyasi/belgeler/233.pdf (last accessed 10 April 2021).

Islamic statecraft. For there are tantalising hints that Bustani's own understanding of the political was shaped by his engagement with this tradition. It is striking, for instance, that he expected ordinary subjects to obey not just the universal norms of religion and morals, but also the specific injunctions of *siyasa*. Now commonly translated as 'politics', this was still in the mid-nineteenth century a polysemic and fluid term, which denoted both statecraft and the administration of justice. It was in this latter sense that it was used in Khedivial Egypt, where *majalis siyasiyya* were established alongside the *shari'a* courts and granted 'discretionary powers' to adjudicate criminal cases using new bureaucratic procedure.[83]

At another level, however, the term evoked a tradition of reflection on statecraft that included both works of counsel for rulers such as the *Qabus-nama* and Nizam al-Mulk's *Siyasat-nama*, both written for eleventh-century Seljuk rulers, and philosophical treatises such as al-Farabi's tenth-century *al-Madina al-Fadila*, the 'ideal city' or *polis*, and Nasir al-Din al-Tusi's thirteenth-century *Akhlaq-i Nasiri*. For al-Farabi, the ultimate end of the 'royal, political art' of *siyasa* was to lead man 'to happiness by having a philosopher-king as ruler'. In Edwin Rosenthal's gloss, the sovereign should 'rule with practical wisdom and experience ... so that political ... acts encourage virtue and good behaviour' in his subjects.[84] In similar fashion, al-Tusi saw the duty of the 'ideal ruler' as being to 'help his subjects' to 'reach potential wisdom'. Under his 'care and protection each member of society, secure in the best place suited for him, was to ... struggle to achieve perfection'. For him, *siyasat-i mudun* – the management of the affairs of the *polis*, or statecraft – was one of the two central expressions of 'practical wisdom' – *hikmat-i 'amali*.[85]

We cannot know for certain whether Bustani had in mind the writings of Farabi and Tusi. As Peter Hill has noted, 'we should not assume that ... particular passages' drawn from the classical canon 'were known to' nineteenth-century 'Arab literati'.[86] More work still needs to be done on *nahda* thinkers' reception of *falsafa*, the tradition born of Islamic engagement with Plato and Aristotle, and the ways this shaped their ideas of ethics, virtue and the state. At the same time, we do know that the sixteenth-century Ottoman writers Kınalızade Ali Çelebi and Hasan Kafi, who drew from Tusi and other medieval Persian writers of ethics their sense of the relationship between wise government and

[83] Khaled Fahmy, *In Quest of Justice: Islamic Law and Forensic Medicine in Modern Egypt* (Oakland, 2018), 83 and 81–131 *passim*.
[84] Edwin Rosenthal, *Political Thought in Medieval Islam: An Introductory Outline* (Cambridge 1958), 119–20.
[85] Muzaffar Alam, *The Languages of Political Islam in India, c.1200–1800* (Ranikhet, 2004), 47–9.
[86] Hill, *Utopia and Civilisation*, 84.

social order, were known to Bustani's contemporaries.[87] Kınalızade's *Ahlak-i Ala'i* was first printed at the Bulaq press in Cairo in 1833 and went through a number of editions over the course of the nineteenth century. Hasan Kafi's work was likewise reprinted three times before 1870.[88] Bustani's near-contemporary the Young Ottoman Namık Kemal cited both Kınalızade and Tusi, among others.[89] Another contemporary, the Tunisian reformer Khayr al-Din al-Tunsi, argued in a passage in which he cited the 'wisdom of Aristotle' that 'the rightful path is 'the statecraft practised by the ruler (*siyasa yasusiha al-malik*)'.[90]

Alongside this we must place the evidence from Bustani's own dictionary, *Muhit al-Muhit*, published seven years after the *Nafir*. There, he gave the meaning of *hukuma* – nowadays glossed as 'government' – as *arbab al-siyasa*, or the masters of statecraft. More telling still, among the definitions of *hikma* or wisdom that he listed were the following: 'justice and learning and understanding and reason (*hilm*) and prophecy and the Qur'an and the Gospels'; and 'the science of the truth of things as they are'. The 'people of wisdom', he went on, 'are the philosophers (*al-falasifa*)', or those who practise *falsafa*, a term often used for thinkers such as al-Farabi and al-Ghazali.[91] We must at least allow for the possibility that when Bustani wrote in the *Nafir* of the 'wisdom of rulers (*hikmat al-amirin*)' and the need to rebuild the trust of 'subjects ... in their government (*hukumatihim*)', he had these meanings and the tradition from which they sprung in mind.[92] More than a thinker gazing forward proleptically into the national future, Bustani appears at such moments to be grappling with this long, rich tradition of reflection on the relationship between reason, ethics and government. If the Tanzimat decrees themselves redeployed this language, as some have argued, we must be open to the possibility that so too did the *Nafir*.[93]

---

[87] See Sariyannis, *Ottoman Political Thought*, 66, 73–4; and Asli Niyazioğlu, 'Kınalızade Ali Efendi', in *Encyclopaedia of Islam III*, https://referenceworks.brillonline.com/entries/encyclopaedia-of-islam-3/knalzade-ali-efendi-COM_35605?s.num=0&s.f.s2_parent=s.f.book.encyclopaedia-of-islam-3&s.q=Kinalizade (last accessed 2 April 2021).

[88] Darling, *History of Social Justice*, 172; Şerif Mardin, *The Genesis of Young Ottoman Thought: A Study in the Modernization of Turkish Political Ideas* (Princeton, 1962), 198. See also H. Z. Ülkan, 'Tanzimattan sonra Fikir Hariketleri', in *Tanzimat I: Yüzüncü Yıldönümü Münasebitile*, ed. H.-A. Yücel (Istanbul, 1940), 774; and M. A. Mehmet, 'La Crise ottomane dans la vision de Hasan Kafi Akhisri (1544–1616)', *Revue des Etudes Sud-Est Européennes*, 13 (1975), 388 n. 27.

[89] Mardin, *Genesis*, 82, 99.

[90] Khayr al-Din al-Tunsi, *Aqwam al-Masalik fi Maʿrafat Ahwal al-Mamalik*, ed. Munsif al-Shanufi (Tunis, 1972), 117.

[91] Butrus al-Bustani, *Kitab Muhit al-Muhit taʾlif al-Muʿallim Butrus al-Bustani ufiya ʿanhu ayya Qamus Mutawwal al-Lugha al-ʿArabiyya* (2 vols., Beirut, 1867), I, 430–1.

[92] Bustani, *Nafir Suriyya*, 45.

[93] Darling, *History of Social Justice*, 162. See also Butrus Abu-Manneh, 'The Islamic Roots of the Gülhane Rescript', *Die Welt des Islams*, 34 (1994), 173–203; Frederick Anscombe, 'Islam and the Age of Ottoman Reform', *Past & Present*, 208 (2010), 159–89.

## VI Looking outwards: global comparison and imperial sovereignty

At other moments, Bustani looked not backwards into tradition, but outwards across the world to find evidence in support of his argument. This is apparent from a passage in November 1860 in which he strove to distinguish between religion, understood as an intrinsically hier-archical relationship between 'a servant and his maker', and civil matters – *al-madaniyyat* – understood as a dual contract, which entailed at once a horizontal relationship between 'man and his compatriot' and a vertical engagement between the individual subject and 'his gov-ernment'. The relationship of one compatriot to another, and between subject and government, were not independent of one another. As Bustani wrote:

> So long as the sons of the country do not open the doors to knowledge and industry ... they cannot wait for order along the lines of civilised countries or respect and consider-ation in the eyes of others, nor even in their own eyes, or expect to have the doors opened to them to lofty positions in government. For though the Arabs were, in times of old, sovereign and possessed the most well-considered positions, it cannot be hoped that they will progress higher than the rank of a scribe or translator or council member should they remain in their current position.

In short, 'the Arabs' owed it to each other to embark on the educational reforms Bustani had long espoused. But if this was in part because it would bring 'order' and civilisation to their own lands, it was also because it would allow them to earn the respect of others and integrate fully the institutions of state. Awakening their latent potentialities, then, meant nothing if it did not strengthen their ties to the imperial polity. At the same time, the Ottoman state itself needed to do more to 'open the doors' of government to all. For 'God only knows how many of the current government employees' would remain, should

> the government create an order like that in the Chinese empire, for example, which does not accept anyone into government functions who is not competent, who does not possess perfect knowledge of the language of his land, and who is not expert in the laws and regulations of the empire.[94]

What are we to make of this comparison, made at a time when, some have argued, Bustani anxiously regarded Western civilisation as the uni-versal benchmark by which all other societies should be judged?[95] To be clear, this was no empirical comparison. As Bustani was writing, much of China had been consumed for a decade by what was, by some reckon-ings, the bloodiest civil war in history. For four years, the Qing state

---

[94] Bustani, *Nafir Suriyya*, 49.
[95] Sheehi, *Foundations*, 12, 14; Makdisi, 'After 1860', 614. For an insightful discussion of this, see Hill, *Utopia and Civilisation*, ch. 2.

had been confronting British and French military incursions. Its coastline was moth-eaten by the extraterritorial enclaves of the treaty ports.[96] But all this was beside the point, for it is clear that Bustani was writing here in the abstract. This passage, then, was fundamentally different from the comparative empirical accounts of Khayr al-Din al-Tunsi or the Egyptian Rif'at Rifa' al-Tahtawi, or even from later Ottoman writings on Meiji Japan.[97] Rather, Bustani saw in a stylised China the ideal type of the bureaucratic empire he longed for. This underscores the continuing openness and worldliness of mid-nineteenth-century Ottoman Arab political thought. Casting about for a normative basis for effective imperial governance, Bustani felt no need to look exclusively to the precedents offered by the 'civilised countries' of Europe and North America. On the contrary, he set his gaze eastwards across the globe.

This effort at global comparison was the product, to be sure, of what Peter Hill has described as Bustani's profound wariness of 'uncritical acceptance' of Europe as the 'universal standard of civilisation' and his fear that his compatriots would lose themselves in 'blind imitation' of 'all things' Western.[98] But if cultural considerations were at play, so too were political ones. As Bustani stressed in February 1861, European powers' growing encroachments on Ottoman sovereignty rendered the task of reforming the state and rebuilding the trust between ruler and ruled all the more urgent. For only through fulfilling the Tanzimat's commitment to 'preserve the peace and comfort and prosperity' of its subjects could the Ottoman state 'convince them there is no need ... to have recourse to foreigners and to place their livelihoods and interests under their protection and supervision'.[99] Here, too, we can feel Bustani's immediate lived context pressing into the text. He wrote, after all, in a city in which those displaced by violence remained reliant on European relief efforts, and in which many profited from the silk trade with France or found

[96] Tobie Meyer-Fong, *What Remains: Coming to Terms with Civil War in Nineteenth-Century China* (Stanford, 2013); James L. Hevia, *English Lessons: The Pedagogy of Imperialism in Nineteenth-Century China* (Durham, NC, 2003). See also Ussama Makdisi, 'Diminished Responsibility and the Impossibility of "Civil War" in the Middle East', *American Historical Review*, 120 (2015), 1739–52.

[97] Rifa'ah Rafi' al-Tahtawi, *An Imam in Paris: Account of a Stay in France by an Egyptian Cleric (1826–1831)*, trans. Daniel L. Newman (2004); Khayr al-Din al-Tunsi, *The Surest Path: The Political Treatise of a Nineteenth-Century Muslim Statesman*, trans. Leon Carl Brown (Cambridge, MA, 1967). On Ottoman views of Japan, see Cemil Aydin, *The Politics of Anti-Westernism in Asia: Visions of World Order in Pan-Islamic and Pan-Asian Thought* (New York, 2007); and Renee Worringer, *Ottomans Imagining Japan: East, Middle East, and Non-Western Modernity at the Turn of the Twentieth Century* (New York, 2014).

[98] Hill, *Utopia and Civilisation*, 114, 112, 115.

[99] Bustani, *Nafir Suriyya*, 59.

employment as dragomans or guards in European employ, as Bustani
had done in the 1840s.[100]

It is clear that despite – or perhaps because of – his earlier entangle-
ments, Bustani retained a deep ambivalence about the role of foreign
powers in Syria. On the one hand, he wrote in January 1861,
European 'intervention' had been 'necessary to stop the spread of
turmoil and destruction that were spreading from place to place ...
like infectious disease'. There was no denying that 'misrule and disdain
for the laws are among the greatest of harms to a country, no matter
what its degree of civilisation and success, as wise government and virtuous laws are like health, one only knows their value when they are lost', so
that 'those who transgress the bounds of humanity and moderation find
themselves facing the opprobrium of the entire world, and it is necessary
for a foreign hand to intervene in the affairs of their country'. On the
other hand,

> interference by foreign hands in the political affairs (*siyasa*) of any country, and especially
> this country, where it strengthened the various conflicting parties ... and where the
> causes of disagreement on the causes of intervention varied in accordance with the reli-
> gious and civil interests of the intervening parties, will be harmful to the country, even if
> it brings temporary benefits to some individuals.[101]

In this passage, Bustani again brought together the normative and
the descriptive, the eventful and the speculative. Intervention in the sovereign matters of any given state, he contended, was always detrimental.
But events had shown that it was especially so in Mount Lebanon
and Syria, where Britain and France had shown contrasting attitudes
towards Druze and Maronite, and where French endorsement of
Maronite claims, in particular, had strengthened the latter's hand.
Gone here is the sense of hopeful gratitude that marked Bustani's first
*wataniyya*, in which he counselled his readers to 'look with trust' on the
'allied states coming to provide them with comfort and to make them
secure in their dwelling places' and 'wait patiently for the good deeds
that the great of the world had set in motion'.[102] By early 1861, this opti-
mism had been replaced by a growing sense of the dangers of foreign
encroachment. If the Ottoman state appeared to him the guarantor of
the welfare of Syria, then the European states that had assembled in
Beirut to decide on the fate of Syria increasingly seemed not saviours
and protectors, but threats to its well-being.

---

[100] See Leila Tarazi Fawaz, *Merchants and Migrants in Nineteenth-Century Beirut* (Cambridge,
MA, 1983); Boutros Labaki, *Introduction à l'Histoire économique du Liban: soie et commerce extérieur en
fin de période ottomane (1840–1914)* (Beirut, 1984); Hanssen, *Fin de Siècle Beirut*.
[101] Bustani, *Nafir Suriyya*, 52.
[102] Ibid., 10.

## VII Conclusion

Butrus al-Bustani's *Nafir Suriyya*, I have argued, can be read not just as a call for a new Syrian patriotism, but as a contemplation on the workings of empire. Bustani reflected at various moments on the imperial ruler's duties and attributes and his subjects' obligations and rights, on the relationship between state and population and capital and province, on the reform of imperial administration, and on the dangers foreign intervention and encroachment posed to Ottoman sovereignty. To do so, he drew not just on the language of the Tanzimat, but also on an older language of ethical statecraft, as well as on comparison with other imperial polities such as China, whose civil administration open to all the talents he saw as a model for bureaucratic governance. At the same time, Bustani offered a commentary on the future of Mount Lebanon. Here too, he stressed the importance of empire. For he counselled not just against a return to the dominance of local elites or an increased role for religious dignitaries in government, but also against the various schemes for autonomous administration floated for the region as he wrote. The only means to overcome the violence of 1860 was, he argued, wholesale integration into the reformed structures of the Tanzimat state, embracing the norms of Ottoman imperial governance rather than carving out an exception under the protection of other, European, empires.

In the end, Bustani's vision did not come to pass. By June 1861, the international commission sitting in Beirut had drawn up the basic law that would regulate Mount Lebanon's government until the First World War. Far from doing away with confessionalism, this document enshrined it as the basis of administrative order: henceforth, the region's governor would be a Christian, assisted by an administrative council made up of representatives of the mountain's religious communities. At the same time, Mount Lebanon would enjoy a significant measure of autonomy, with its own gendarmerie and fiscal system. This autonomy would be 'guaranteed' by the concert of powers, which thus gained a significant measure of oversight over its internal affairs.[103] Though this arrangement ensured a 'long peace' for Ottoman Mount Lebanon, it also allowed for continuing French and British intervention in its political life and the entrenchment of the logic of confessional government.[104] Bustani's writings, then, offer an alternative future – one that provides grounds for further reflection on

---

[103] Adel Ismail, *Documents Diplomatiques et consulaires relatifs à l'histoire du Liban et des pays du proche-orient, du XVIIe siècle à nos jours* (20 vols., Beirut, 1975–), XI, 102–11.

[104] Engin Akarlı, *The Long Peace: Ottoman Lebanon, 1861–1920* (1993). See also John Spagnolo, *France and Ottoman Lebanon, 1861–1914* (1977).

the ways late-Ottoman Arab literati reckoned with the existence of empire and on the relationship between lived and textual contexts and the relationship between political engagement and normative prescription. These are the grounds that I have tried to open up here.

Recent years have seen a revival of interest in Bustani. The last decade alone has witnessed important work by the likes of Rana Issa, Nadia Bou Ali, Peter Hill, Ussama Makdisi, and Jens Hanssen and Hicham Safieddine, whose critical edition provides English-language readers with access to the *Nafir*. This interest is in part the product of an enduring fascination with the complexities and paradoxes of Bustani's thought – and of the *nahda* more broadly – and of its complicated influence on subsequent generations of Arab thinkers. But it is also an attempt to push back against enduring Western narratives of the Middle East as a place of disorder and fanaticism, to demonstrate, once and for all, that it was not always thus, that confessionalism and sectarianism are historical constructs, mutable, motile practices amenable to context and not the fixed fittings of Arab society, and that there exists a rich tradition of what Ussama Makdisi has recently called 'ecumenical' or 'antisectarian' thought in the region.[105] Understandably, then, many of these writings – even when critical of the contradictions in his thinking – have taken Bustani's chief concern to be the *patria* and the horizontal ties of concord and understanding binding the inhabitants of a shared homeland together. They are not wrong. Patriotism was integral to his political thought. But it is perhaps time that we also read Bustani as a thinker of empire, one who was also concerned with the vertical ties between imperial state and subject, with the ethical and practical underpinnings of imperial governance, and with the conditions of imperial sovereignty and the increasingly stark power asymmetries between imperial polities. In doing so, we may be true both to the context in which these haunting, allusive texts took shape and to our own tragic times of intervention and unequal sovereignty.

---

[105] Makdisi, *Age of Coexistence*. See also Hanssen and Safieddine, 'Translating Civil War', 1–2.

*Transactions of the RHS* 31 (2021), pp. 115–122 © The Author(s), 2021. Published by Cambridge University Press on behalf of the Royal Historical Society. This is an Open Access article, distributed under the terms of the Creative Commons Attribution licence (https://creativecommons.org/licenses/by/4.0/), which permits unrestricted re-use, distribution, and reproduction in any medium, provided the original work is properly cited.
doi:10.1017/S0080440121000062

# REVISITING RHS'S 'RACE, ETHNICITY & EQUALITY IN UK HISTORY: A REPORT AND RESOURCE FOR CHANGE'

## By Shahmima Akhtar

ABSTRACT. This paper considers the Royal Historical Society (RHS)'s 'Race, Ethnicity & Equality in UK History' report published in 2018. The report contained the findings of a survey sent to staff and students working or studying in History higher education in the United Kingdom. In this paper, I reflect on the various findings of the report related to staff and student numbers, the attainment gap between white and Black and Ethnic Minority students, the curriculum, and racial harassment in History within universities. The RHS report emerged out of the work done by a number of organisations championing race and equality in the sector over decades. By connecting the work of RHS to these earlier initiatives it is possible to map a broader societal change in the historical sector to address historic inequalities, racialised disadvantage and structural exclusion. The RHS and institutions such as Runnymede Trust, the Institute of Historical Research, and Leading Routes are championing greater racial and ethnic equality which reflects broader political, economic and cultural transformations taking place in Britain. In this paper, I show how the RHS is part of an important conversation in foregrounding racial and ethnic equality in the historical profession to the inevitable benefit of History higher education.

It has been almost three years since the publication of 'Race, Ethnicity & Equality in UK History: A Report and Resource for Change'.[1] The Royal Historical Society (RHS)'s Race, Ethnicity and Equality Working Group (REEWG) established in 2017 produced the Race Report, and its members (old and new) are still active in this space. The report offered a survey of History in higher education, detailing that History is the fifth least diverse subject in UK universities in

---

[1] RHS received around 730 surveys, completed by staff and students in History varying from undergraduates and early career researchers to permanent salaried and professorial level. Responses contained rich qualitative material in the free text boxes (amounting to over 100 pages of commentary).

terms of race and ethnicity.[2] Specifically, the report found that under-graduate-level History had an overwhelmingly white student population, that the numbers of BME students were even lower when it came to post-graduate-level History and specifically that 'History academic staff are less diverse than Historical & Philosophical Studies student cohorts, with 93.7 per cent of History staff drawn from White backgrounds, and only 0.5 per cent Black, 2.2 per cent Asian and 1.6 per cent Mixed.'[3] Since the publication of the report, there have been many events, meetings and workshops held by history departments throughout universities in the United Kingdom. The discussions invariably responded to a climate of change; a growing recognition of the pervasive inequalities within History higher education; and ultimately a desire to do something about it.

The Black Lives Matter movement originated in the United States, but its impact has been keenly felt throughout the world, including the United Kingdom, and England specifically.[4] Global protests against police violence, structural racism and white supremacy are a regular feature of our everyday politics. The movement encompasses everything from calling attention to statues of slave-owners to demanding that the curriculum no longer be white-centric. Cumulatively, these activists, young people and protesters are demanding a change to the inbuilt mechanics of racism that affect our daily lives, whether in our institu-tions, our education systems, our financial programmes, or else systems of language and knowledge. Inequality along racial, ethnic as well as gen-dered and sexuality lines is commonplace and inescapable. In response to growing calls to reconsider, re-evaluate and retell the story of Britain's empire, a right-wing backlash has grown in earnest. In June 2020 a Conservative think tank, Policy Exchange, launched a monitoring project called 'History Matters' which 'confirms that history is the most active front in a new culture war' and tracks institutions that have taken steps to remove statues, rename buildings or update univer-sity curricula. Ultimately, systematic recognition of institutionalised

---

[2] Shahmima Akhtar, 'Racism, Redistribution, Redress: Royal Historical Society and "Race, Ethnicity & Equality in UK History: A Report and Resource for Change"', in *British Culture after Empire: Migration, Race and Decolonisation, 1945 to the Present*, ed. Liam Liburd, Emma Parker and Josh Doble (Manchester, forthcoming).

[3] 'Race, Ethnicity & Equality in UK History: A Report and Resource for Change' (October 2018), p. 8. I use the term Black and Minority Ethnic (BME) throughout this paper, to ensure consistency with the statistical data on race in higher education whilst being aware of its conceptual limitations. The Higher Education Statistics Agency (HESA) classifies History, Archaeology, Heritage Studies, Philosophy and Theology and Religious Studies as one student category in its data sets.

[4] Wesley Lowery, *They Can't Kill Us All: Ferguson, Baltimore, and a New Era in America's Racial Justice Movement* (2016).

racism has moved people by the tens of thousands to demand that we no longer have monuments celebrating slave-owners, that we no longer avoid teaching histories of the British Empire, that we recognise that racism has real-world effects.

Importantly, the Race Report built on previous studies that have extensively documented the sustained racial and ethnic inequalities inbuilt within UK universities. The Black and Asian Studies network, the Young Historians Project, the efforts of the Institute of Commonwealth Studies, the teaching resources of the Arts and Humanities Research Council (AHRC)-funded Runnymede Trust project 'Our Migration Story: The Making of Modern Britain' and the Institute of Historical Research's 'Teaching British Histories of Race, Migration and Empire', as well as the Museum Detox network, framed and continue to frame the RHS's and REEWG's work. They have led the sector in not only collecting qualitative and quantitative data on racial and ethnic inequality but also coming up with innovative pedagogical, research and methodological approaches to counter the inaccessibility of history to BME groups. For instance, resources from lesson plans to bibliographies of secondary sources, and archival material, as well as safe spaces are offered by the above networks.[5] These networks are responding to reports published concurrently with or in the aftermath of the RHS report. Specifically, there have been reports on the awarding gap and the experience of racial harassment, and 'Leading Routes: The Broken Pipeline' presented specific data on 'Black PhD Students Accessing Research Council Funding'. It found that over a three-year period, of the total of 19,868 Ph.D. funded studentships awarded by UK Research and Innovation (UKRI) research councils collectively, 245 (1.2 per cent) were awarded to Black or Black Mixed students, just 30 of whom were from Black Caribbean backgrounds (UKRI, 2019).[6] The cumulative efforts of this range of

[5] See 'Ethnicity, Race and Inequality in the UK: State of the Nation', Report by Runnymede, Ethnicity UK and Policy Press (2020); Mia Liyanage, 'Miseducation: Decolonising Curricula, Culture and Pedagogy in UK Universities', Higher Education Policy Institute Report (July 2020); Equality and Human Rights Commission, 'Tackling Racial Harassment: Universities Challenged' (2019); Nicola Rollock, '"Staying Power": The Career Experiences and Strategies of UK Black Female Professors', University and College Union Report (February 2019); Universities UK/National Union of Students, 'Black, Asian and Minority Ethnic Student Attainment at UK Universities: #CLOSINGTHEGAP' (May 2019); Mohammed Ishaq and Asifa Maaria Hussain, 'BAME Staff Experiences of Academic and Research Libraries', SCONUL Report (June 2019); Runnymede Trust, 'Teaching Migration, Belonging, and Empire in Secondary Schools' (July 2019); Sofia Akel, 'Insider–Outsider: The Role of Race in Shaping the Experiences of Black and Minority Ethnic Students' (October 2019).
[6] 'Leading Routes: The Broken Pipeline – Barriers to Black PhD Students Accessing Research Council Funding' (September 2019), p. 3.

organisations paved the way for RHS's report to be welcomed in the historical sector.

With respect to higher education History, the RHS report found that, at undergraduate level, 11 per cent of historical and philosophical students are BME, despite BME students making up 23 per cent of the overall UK undergraduate population.[7] Further, at postgraduate level, 17 per cent of all UK students come from a BME background, but within historical and philosophical studies departments this drops to 9 per cent. There are varied reasons for these numbers, a key one being the curriculum: the report identified that history curriculum content from secondary school level to university diminished interest in History amongst BME students. Several institutions have instituted curriculum reviews as a result, prompted by campaigns such as 'Why Is my Curriculum So White?'. As part of this, history departments are engaging meaningfully with efforts to diversify reading lists in the first instance, with a longer-term aim of decolonising course content and course material. Importantly, colleagues should avoid such efforts that focus just on discrete courses, which are only one piece of the puzzle. Whilst changing a particular course is within an academic's control, equal attention should be paid to making survey and compulsory courses far more diverse, as students will inevitably be exposed to a broader range of teaching on a mandatory level.

There is a vast literature on racism and higher education that has guided these efforts, including Katy Sian, *Navigating Institutional Racism in British Universities* (2019); Lola Olufemi, Odelia Younge, Waithera Sebatindira and Suhaiymah Manzoor-Khan, *A FLY Girl's Guide To University: Being a Woman of Colour at Cambridge and Other Institutions of Elitism and Power* (2019); and Jason Arday and Heidi Safia Mirza (eds.), *Dismantling Race in Higher Education: Racism, Whiteness and Decolonising the Academy* (2018). For those of us who are willing to do the work of improving racial and ethnic equality in History higher education, the above texts are useful guides to the state of the field and provide actionable points of intervention. For RHS, specifically, in order to map the impact of the report, the society published 'Roadmap for Change' in 2019, and a follow-up Roadmap in 2020 which summarises how universities, learned societies and a variety of institutions have responded to the report and its findings. Both these reports contain useful examples of how different institutions have actioned the recommendations of the report, as well as lessons learnt from it.

When we begin to break down the data on staff in history departments, who are 94 per cent white, we can see that whilst 6 per cent

---

[7] 'Race Report', p. 22.

come from a BME background, only 0.5 per cent are black.[8] The report specifically found that the numerically limited BME staff and students in History higher education experience a discriminatory and exclusionary working environment. For instance, 44 per cent of BME respondents faced problems with unconscious or implicit bias around race and ethnicity. Thirty-three per cent of BME respondents reported witnessing discrimination or abuse of staff and students based on race and ethnicity. Further, 30 per cent of respondents reported having experienced such discrimination or abuse themselves. Finally, most discrimination or abuse was at the hands of staff within their own department, and the rest was by students or the public.[9] These statistics point to the fact that representation alone will not fix issues of racism, as the few students and academics of colour who do make it into History higher education still suffer abuse. Nowhere is this more clearly visible than in the attainment gap. This is now more accurately referred to as the 'awarding gap', to recognise the role of academics in sustaining this inequality.[10] For example, the RHS report found that BME students and white students are equally likely to get a 2.1 but BME students are 9 per cent less likely to get a first than a white student.[11] A primary next step for addressing this academy-wide awarding gap is to ask for specific department-level data on the awarding gap in order to come up with next steps, whether it be bespoke staff-training on equality, diversity and inclusivity (EDI) and the attainment gap, resourcing further support for BME students, or else raising awareness of the topic.

A small yet effective change that institutions can adopt based on a recommendation of the Race Report is to make EDI a standing item on agendas for department-, school- and college-level meetings. This ensures that there is a space for discussion and an opportunity to move forward and update colleagues on the adjustments or changes that are needed for successful EDI initiatives.

Whilst it is largely positive that universities, whether on a department or college level, are engaging with the many reports on racial inequality in our education systems and specifically universities, we must continue efforts to be anti-racist. Historian Meleisa Ono-George has discussed an anti-racist pedagogy, which is an understanding of racism as historically and socially constructed, embedded, and normalised within modern

---

[8] *Ibid.*, p. 8.

[9] *Ibid.*, pp. 54–5.

[10] L. Sequeira, 'Three Unis Discuss What They're Doing about the Attainment Gap', *LSE Blog*, 9 May 2019.

[11] Race Report', p. 40. Debra Cureton, 'Bridging the BME Gap' (April 2016), and Kingston University have continued RHS's sector-leading work in closing the BME attainment gap through an externally funded Office for Students project.

society. Ono-George conceives of universities as sites of knowledge production, that are partially responsible for unequal dynamics of power in society given that 'all education is political'; an anti-racist pedagogy therefore encourages students to be reflexive, active participants, and engaged in collaborative learning, which extends beyond the lecture theatre and into the outside world.[12]

Over successive years, many public history practitioners have done much to bring the debates on Britain's history and racial equality into conversation with one another. David Olusoga's work on Black British history, published as a monograph, screened as a documentary series and even turned into a children's book, has brought Black British history to mainstream, not just specialised, audiences.[13] Afua Hirsch, Akala and Renei-Eddo Lodge have respectively published on the ways in which Britishness intersects with black identity in the discourse of race and injustice in contemporary Britain.[14] Many have pointed to the relative silence on histories of race, migration and empire as fuelling continued injustices that refuse Britain's black and brown populace a place in British history. Failing to teach these histories perpetuates a false narrative of Britain that fails to consider the interconnectedness of the British Empire, the networks of food, culture, society and religions that have been present historically and continue to adapt and change today. By sidelining this history, not only are a whole generation of potential future black and brown historians being consigned to the margins of the history academy, whether at primary or secondary school or at university, but these young people are also being sidelined to the margins of British citizenship and British society. A more composite and holistically considered approach that considers the diversity of human experience across historical generations needs to be actualised. These vanguards of the historical profession are sustaining the societal conditions necessary for equalities work such as that of the RHS and some universities to thrive.

Localised networks of solidarity exist for BME historians, such as the Young Historians Project, the BME Social History Network, Leading Routes and more. These networks provide spaces for discussion, connection and collaboration, but ultimately a generative existence in academia needs to go beyond survival. As Toni Morrison thoughtfully expounded in a talk at Portland State University (PSU) in 1975:

---

[12] Meleisa Ono-George, '"Power in the Telling": Community-Engaged Histories of Black Britain', *History Workshop Online*, 18 November 2019: www.historyworkshop.org.uk/power-in-the-telling.

[13] David Olusoga, *Black and British: A Forgotten History* (2016).

[14] Afua Hirsch, *Brit(ish): On Race, Identity and Belonging* (New York, 2018); Akala, *Natives: Race and Class in the Ruins of Empire* (London, 2018); Reni Eddo-Lodge, *Why I'm No Longer Talking to White People about Race* (2017).

The function, the very serious function of racism is distraction. It keeps you from doing your work. It keeps you explaining, over and over again, your reason for being. Somebody says you have no language, and you spend twenty years proving that you do. Somebody says your head isn't shaped properly so you have scientists working on the fact that it is. Somebody says you have no art, so you dredge that up. Somebody says you have no kingdoms, so you dredge that up. None of this is necessary. There will always be one more thing.[15]

Considering Morrison's astute remarks, how do those engaged in improving the historical sector go about equality, diversity and inclusivity work without being perpetually distracted – from our academic work, our articles that need to come out, our books that need to be published, our courses that need to be designed? It seems that EDI work functions as a double-edged sword – both acting as a necessary corrective to generations of injustice, minoritisation and harassment but further serving to abstract those people of colour engaged in these initiatives as inevitably distracted or else siloed as being exclusively interested in race and equality work. What of their research interests, their academic outputs and their career progression? Promotion criteria of course take into account administrative responsibilities, including EDI, but when this work requires emotional as well as physical labour, the cumulative effort cannot be quantified or monetised. Ultimately, the people engaged in this work are doing it because they care, because they want to change higher education for the better in the long term, or else change their working and learning environment, whether at department or school level, in the short term. There is no clear answer as to how this work is to be done equitably, beyond working in collaboration with colleagues and co-curating with students. In essence, it will take a toll on one's performance and outputs, but good EDI work engages in the three R's as Dr Jonathan Saha put it: it needs to be Rewarded, Recognised and Resourced.[16] These three R's demonstrate serious commitment whilst recognising individual and group effort. Recent examples of positive work in the historical sector range from the flurry of posts in Black British History, to the use of positive action in ring-fencing Ph.D. and Masters funding, to small grants for BME historians (funded by a range of history scholarly societies), to name a few.

In conclusion, the Race Report does not exist in isolation from broader societal changes. Importantly, the 2011 Census showed that just under 20 per cent of the UK's population self-identified as other than White British, while the UK's Black and Minority Ethnic

[15] PSU address transcribed by film-maker Ava DuVernay, which can be accessed at www.wweek.com/news/2019/08/07/one-of-late-writer-toni-morrisons-most-famous-quotes-about-racism-came-from-a-talk-at-portland-state-university-listen-to-it-here

[16] Jonathan Saha, 'A Response to Critics', *History Workshop Online*, 30 October 2018: www.historyworkshop.org.uk/the-rhs-race-ethnicity-equality-report-a-response-to-critics.

population doubled in size between 1991 and 2011, to eight million people (14 per cent of the overall population).[17] In recognition of Britain's multicultural, multiethnic, and multinational population, there is a need to underscore equality in our lives if only guided by the Equality Act of 2010. The discourse on race is changing in Britain, and its citizens are joining the call of generations before us that are no longer willing to allow racism to continue unabated, to see it as the work of singular 'bad apples' or else the eccentricities of older individuals (despite what our public press might tell us).[18] The history academy is in conversation with these broader discourses and we must continue to be reflexive in order to remain rigorous in practice, and relevant to the changing landscape of the British nation. History matters now more than ever before, and we must continue to fight for history that is diverse, honest and accountable.

---

[17] Bridget Byrne, Claire Alexander, Omar Khan, James Nazroo and William Shankley (eds.), *Ethnicity, Race and Inequality in the UK: State of the Nation* (Bristol, 2020), p. 9.

[18] See Luke Harding, 'The Chequered Legacy of Prince Philip's Notorious "Gaffes"', *The Guardian*, 11 April 2021, for a particularly egregious example of Prince Philip's racist remarks being whitewashed as humorous quips.